"No one 'floats' into spiritual maturity. They create intention and live with intentionality to grow, acting on that intention habitually and joyfully. Adam Kareus is my friend and co-laborer in the local church, and in *Decided* he lays out various aspects of living the Christian faith with intentionality. The gospel of Christ is central to Adam's life, preaching, and writing. If you want to focus on the gospel and live it well, read on!"

—Dr. Phillip McClure,
Lead Pastor of River Valley Community Church,
Fort Smith, Arkansas

"Too many people are living life by accident. They are going whichever way their circumstances push them, without any thought toward the life God is calling them to live. In his book *Decided*, Adam Kareus invites us to a different way. Intention, not apathy, should rule our lives as we seek to live in a way that honors God. With a pastor's heart and a scholar's brain, Adam shows us how to live with intention."

—Kevin A. Thompson,
Lead Pastor of Community Bible Church,
Fort Smith, Arkansas;
author of *Friends, Partners, and Lovers*

"When I met Adam eight years ago, we were friends first and later became colleagues. Finally, and most importantly, he became a pastor to me in one of the most difficult seasons of my life. Over the course of our friendship, I learned that when Adam speaks, I listen . . . and when he writes, I read. That is why I am overjoyed he chose to put pen to paper and write this book for us. With a pastor's heart, Adam gives us believers a book that is approachable, concise, and, most importantly, applicable in a way that will encourage you. Furthermore, with a scholar's mind, Adam skillfully handles God's word in a way that will challenge you. Finally, as a lover of Christ and His gospel, Adam joins you on the journey to serve God, the church, and the world in a way that will inspire you. However you chose to read this book, be it alone devotionally or as a part of your small group ministry, I know you'll find a book that will serve you well. Above all, I know you will come to learn what I have: that when Adam Kareus writes, you read."

—Joel Reynolds,
pastor, Hope Church, Franklin, Tennessee;
hospice and National Guard chaplain

DECIDED

LIVING A BIG LIFE FOR CHRIST

ADAM KAREUS

CLAY BRIDGES
PRESS

First Printing 2017

ISBN-10: 1632961164
ISBN-13: 9781632961167
eISBN-10: 1632961172
eISBN-13: 9781632961174

Special Sales: Most Clay Bridges Press titles are available in special quantity discounts. Custom imprinting or excerpting can also be done to fit special needs. Contact Clay Bridges Press at info@lucidbooks.net.

This book is dedicated to Kacee.
Thanks for always believing in me
and being there for me.

TABLE OF CONTENTS

PART 3: THE HOW

INTRODUCTION

intentional: in·ten·tion·al

adjective: done on purpose; deliberate. *Synonyms:* deliberate, calculated, conscious, intended, planned, meant, studied, knowing, willful, purposeful, premeditated, preplanned, preconceived.

How much of your life is planned? How much thought have you put into your day? your week? your year? If you are like most people, you might respond, "Some." You have thought through some goals you want to achieve; you might have a to-do list for the day or week or even month. The big items, the major events and tasks, are thought about; but that is as far as it goes.

The fact of the matter is that most people don't really think through their lives past the big events and major tasks set before them. They don't think through what they are taking in through media on their downtime. They don't think through the small stuff, such as how they are going to spend those few minutes here and there. They don't think through planning interactions with others; they just happen.

And it is understandable. To spend energy thinking through every single item and moment sounds exhausting. If you are like me, it sounds like one more thing we should be doing, and won't end up doing, and it will go into the big pile of guilt of a life not lived "good enough."

But if we had a framework or some way of processing life, we could quickly evaluate and move toward living intentionally in every aspect of our lives. And we do have that: we have the gospel, which provides us with a framework. So instead of being energy-intensive, this task becomes a simple question: "Is what I am doing/thinking/feeling in alignment with the gospel of Jesus Christ?" And that is what this is about.

Have you ever seen young children get into trouble? I have several nephews who always manage to get into trouble. One hits the other, and when asked why he did it, his answer is almost always the same: "I don't know."

All too often, we do the same thing. We do something with consequences, and when faced with the question of why, respond, "I don't know." But if we were to check ourselves and our motives, maybe we would be in a position to know the answer. Better yet, we may be able to stop ourselves from doing things that are contrary to what we believe.

I think J.I. Packer's words fit us all: "I am a sinner who is gifted, or cursed, with ability to talk better than he lives."[1] And this is what I think living for Christ means. It is what I think Jesus means when he calls us to "Follow me." Following Christ isn't just for Sunday mornings, Bible studies, or Christian groups. It is for everyday actions, all decisions and motives, and all of life. So, let's stumble together on this journey to living all of our lives intentionally for Christ.

---

1. Leland Ryken and J.I. Packer, *An Evangelical Life* (Wheaton, IL: Crossway, 2015), 211.

Part 1

THE NEED

Chapter 1

ZOMBIES

I love zombie movies. I can't help it. I know that most of them are pretty bad, not just in a cinema evaluation kind of way but also in content. But I still like them. There is something about the struggle for survival that draws me in. I imagine what I would do in the character's shoes and think about what decisions I would make.

I can almost justify my liking of the zombie genre by making a case that they present great ethical and moral dilemmas. The movies and shows depict society as collapsing, or collapsed, and now you have to survive. They raise the question, "What would you do to survive?" From that angle, they can be a cool tool for a morality exercise. What is the value of human life? Whom are you responsible to?

But zombies provide a great deal of social commentary as well. This was made most famous by the movie *Shaun of the Dead*. The opening scenes show people drifting through life, doing the same things. When they become zombies, not that much changes. And when we take a moment to look at our life, we can see the truth this movie is putting forth.

The fact of the matter is that we all have a tendency to be zombies—some more so than others. Just take a look at zombies and how they live and act. You can see many similarities with our lives. Most people have a tendency to coast through life. They don't desire to work, they really don't have long-term goals, and if they do have goals, they don't know how to achieve them. They have no purpose or ambition driving them or guiding them. I can see this in many people that I went to school with and that I have worked with in ministry. They are coasting, drifting, and living life as it comes. There are even movies and characters that idealize this concept: don't be driven; just float. And that is what zombies do. They stay there, stumbling around until they come across something. They have no purpose, no plan, and no motivation but to drift.

In 2 Thessalonians 3:6, it says, "In the name of the Lord Jesus Christ, we command you, brothers, to keep away from every brother who is idle and does not live according to the teaching you received from us." The rest of the passage talks about people who don't work, but rather live on the generosity of others, justifying it by thinking the end is coming soon. But as Paul writes, to live idly is to violate the teachings of the gospel and our faith.

Zombies also are braindead. They don't think or process; they just do. The humans running from them are thinking about how to survive, but zombies just chase, follow, and don't think. And so many of us have put our brain on the shelf and have stopped thinking as well. We don't truly think through life choices, such as how we spend our money or what the entertainment we are watching is putting into our minds, or how our actions are communicating what we truly believe about life and other people. We are like zombies, living life without processing *why* and *what for*. We know that we are supposed to think about our faith—that is what Jesus implies when He says to love the Lord your God with all your mind (Matt. 22:37).

The enemy wants us to shut down our minds and give no thought to how we are living. According to 2 Corinthians 4:4, "The god of this age has blinded the minds of unbelievers, so that they cannot see the light of the gospel of the glory of Christ, who is the image of God." Unbelievers have blinded minds, but we who know Christ can see. So what is our excuse for not using the amazing gift of a mind enlightened by God?

One last thing about zombies is that they live to feed, something far too often true about us as well. They are controlled by their lust, desire, and hunger. And so often, we are as well. We let our desires control us. We allow the things of this world and the things of the flesh run our life, without worrying or caring what they do to our soul. If you're honest with yourself, you can see this. We gravitate toward that which is comfortable. We seek that which makes us feel good. And these are not always bad, but when they are the controlling drive of our life without any thought toward consequences, then we have become zombies.

For when we were controlled by the sinful nature, the sinful passions aroused by the law were at work in our bodies, so that we bore fruit for death.
—Rom. 7:5

At one time we too were foolish, disobedient, deceived and enslaved by all kinds of passions and pleasures.
—Tit. 3:3

These two verses show how being controlled by our hunger is a characteristic of someone who doesn't know Christ.

A Christ-follower has self-control and can put off following his or her passion for the sake of Christ.

Sometimes, after a long day, I just want to come home, plop on the couch, and "veg out." I have a desire to not think but be idle and let the soothing mindlessness of the TV wash over me. I am willing to bet that there are many of you who feel the same way. In fact, if you'll look at the statistics on average number of hours spent watching TV, you'll see that maybe it's most people. But we were made for so much more than that.

Let's take a look at this phrase "veg out." Such a phrase should never describe me or you or any human. We are not vegetables, we are humans. We are not plants; we are made in the image of God and given the great task and responsibility of being the risen Christ's ambassadors. When we look at what it means to be human, we can see that "vegging out" is really not something that fits.[2]

In Genesis, humans were given a mandate to work. We were given a task: "God blessed them and said to them, be fruitful and increase in number; fill the earth and subdue it. Rule over the fish of the sea and the birds of the air and over every living creature that moves on the ground" (Gen. 1:28). Humans were given work. We were not made for vacation. Some of us think that vacation is how it should be, and that when God made Adam and Eve and said it was good, he was talking about some lifelong vacation. No, there were tasks and work already demanded of them. And we still have the mandate to work.

In fact, those of us who know Christ have not only a

---

2. Douglas Groothuis, a professor I had the honor of learning under at Denver Seminary, first introduced this concept to me.

mandate to work, but also a mission. We will take a look at what this looks like more in later chapters.

When we don't live intentionally, we don't just have a tendency to be like zombies, we *are* zombies. Ephesians 2:1–3 paints the picture of us being dead in our sins and transgressions before we obtain new life in Christ. We were the walking dead, following our zombie desires and the cravings of our sinful natures. "Zombies are not, after all, the only creatures that are walking dead. Spiritual death is the born predicament of every person on the planet."[3]

But thanks be to God that the story doesn't end there. For unlike in movies about zombies, there is a cure, and that cure is the grace of God. The same passage that tells us that we are dead (Eph. 2) goes on in verse 4 to tell us that God made us alive by His grace. But even being made alive, this old way of drifting like a zombie clings to us. It's a fight we must make daily.

---

3. Daniel Montgomery and Timothy Paul Jones, *Proof: Finding Freedom through the Intoxicating Joy of Irresistible Grace* (Grand Rapids: Zondervan, 2014), 48.

Chapter 2

DRIFT AWAY

I love going to the beach. Who doesn't? Vacations can be fun, especially if you can get time to just sit and relax. Beaches tend to be places where that is not only allowed, but expected. Just sit back, crash on a beach chair under an umbrella, and take it easy. Crack open a cold one of whatever suits your fancy, and chill. Let your mind drift off into that peaceful numbness that is in between wake and sleep. Perfectly normal for vacations—and, unfortunately, perfectly normal for many people's everyday life.

This is hard to see, because we are experts in making ourselves look busy and on-task. The average American knows how to make his boss think he is working, and working hard. We know how to put on the mask of diligence and productivity, all the while having our minds resting in that nice, peaceful, near-sleep state. And when our minds rest, our lives will follow.

So we must keep our minds from drifting into that state.

We must keep our minds anchored in something. We must intentionally push and point our minds in the right direction, the direction that we want our lives to follow. The Bible tells us this. In Hebrews 2:1, we see the writer acknowledging that humans' minds have a tendency to drift away: "We must pay more careful attention, therefore, to what we have heard, so that we do not drift away."

I once kayaked in Hawaii to a small island. It was a surreal experience, being in such a picture-perfect locale, doing something people see on the Travel Channel. My parents had taken me to see my brother, who was stationed in Hawaii when he was in the Marines.

If you have ever been around boats and pulling them up on the beach, no matter the location, you know that you have to pull them up enough so that the waves and tide don't get ahold of them. A boat that is loosely anchored will drift away. It is a slow process, one that is even sometimes hard to see. But little-by-little, the water starts lifting, and the boat starts drifting. Before you know it, you might have lost the boat to the ocean.

And if we don't pay attention, as Hebrews says, we will drift away from where we should be planted. We will drift away from what we have heard and believe about Jesus. We will drift away on the tide and current of our culture, away from the grounding that comes from the Gospel. If we don't watch it and pay attention, one day we will look up and realize that we have drifted out to sea and are totally lost.

So pay attention! Employ your mind for Christ, think and ponder on Christ, grab hold of Christ with all of who you are. Because if you were drifting away from land, you would for sure be grabbing hold of the beach with all your might, digging your nails in until they bled, so that you could live.

If you have found yourself drifting, what do you do? Hebrews 6:19 describes the hope we have in God's promise as being an anchor for our soul: "We have this hope as an anchor for the soul, firm and secure." We need that anchor to keep us from drifting out to sea. We need that anchor to keep us grounded on what gives us life.

Grab hold of that anchor and never let go. Pay attention so that you will not continue to drift. These are intentional actions, meaning that they will not happen on their own. We must put them into practice, think through what we are doing, and live with intent.

On our last beach vacation, my brother and I were playing in the waves when we decided to do a scientific test. In movies and TV shows, we always see people in shipwrecks or plane wrecks washing up on a beach of an island. We wanted to test this out. So there we were, two grown men with families, acting like we were passed out in the waves, waiting to see if the waves would wash us up onto the beach. Hey, it was for science.

The only thing that I learned was that drifting in surf is painful. Painful? Yes, painful. What we didn't figure on was that a constant push from the waves would rub us against the sand of the beach, again and again. It didn't feel good, it wasn't relaxing, and it was not a good time. The same is true about drifting through life.

Many people have bought into the lie that drifting is fun in the sun. When they think about drifting, they imagine the lazy river at a water park, where you calmly float around in a big circle. But that is a fixed, contrived, artificial environment. People have intentionally made it safe and comfortable. To drift in real life is to be constantly dragged across the sand of this world, where you have no control and only hope (vainly) that you will wash up somewhere good.

Is that what you want your life to be?

Or would you rather be anchored to a God who loves you and has a plan and purpose for you?

Part 2

THE CALL

Chapter 3

STIMULATE

I have often heard people say, "That was a stimulating conversation," after they have disengaged from a conversation in which they were forced to think. They are basically saying that conversing with that person or group forced them into action or forced them to use their minds in ways that they might not have been used to. In all honesty, I crave stimulating conversation. I crave it to the point that I have little patience with small talk and the fluff that so much of our communication is. Think back to your school years, and I bet that your greatest teachers and professors had this same ability: they had stimulating classes. These are classes in which you had to process information and your mind was forced into another gear to analyze and synthesize the teacher's information.

When I googled the word *stimulate*, I found three definitions. The first was "to raise the levels of physiological or nervous activity in the body." While that can also be good stimulation, that is not what I am talking about here. The second one was "to encourage interest or activity in a person." That is more in line with what I am addressing. When that is combined with the third definition, I think we get the picture: "to encourage development of or increased activity in a state." While the third definition is not pointed at people, I think when we combine the last two, we get at what we all desire. We want to be stimulated in such a way that our interests are piqued. This will encourage an increase in our activity as well.

In the last chapter, I brought up that idea that humans have a tendency to drift. On our own, we take the path of least resistance, or we try to squeak by. You just have to hang out with some teenagers for a while to see this in action. In my many years in youth ministry, this was present again and again. This is not to pick on the youth in our churches or communities—I think they just try to hide it less than adults do, or maybe they haven't learned how to disguise it.

It is to this natural, sliding tendency that the Bible speaks of the responsibility each one of us has to those in our lives. I was reading 2 Peter for my devotional time recently when one word translated two different ways caught my interest. In 2 Peter 1:13, it says, "I think it is right to *refresh* your memory as long as I live in the tent of this body." The word *refresh* here carries the connotation of "to stir up" or "stimulate." So Peter is really saying that he thinks it right for him to stimulate the Christ-followers' memories or to stir them up about what Christ has done. Why would Peter have to do this or think this was needed? Because we have a tendency to drift and forget what Christ has done. We need our minds and memory stimulated so that it can be fresh on them.

This same word is used again in 2 Peter 3:1: "Dear friends, this is now my second letter to you. I have written both of them as reminders to *stimulate* you to wholesome thinking." There is that same word again. Peter knew that one of the big purposes of his writing was to stimulate these Christians to think the right way. Peter also knew that this was important because of our natural tendency to drift away. In fact, just a few verses later, he warns of those who "scoff" and don't believe. We have to stimulate one another back toward the truth so that we don't drift into that group.

While it is a different word, I think this also relates to Hebrews 10:24, which says, "And let us consider how we may *spur* one another toward love and good deeds." This carries much the same connotation as the word used in 2 Peter. We need others to spur us on, but we too often want to do our own thing. The only problem is that, when we do our own thing, we are going against God, and that ultimately will never end well. We need one another to spur us in the direction we need to go. We need one another to stimulate us, to refresh the truth in our memories, to help us have an increase in the right direction.

How can we spur one another on? How can we stimulate one another in this fashion? Psalm 32:8, 9 sheds some light on it. In this Psalm, God says that He will instruct us and teach us in the way we should go and warns us not to be like the horse or mule who must be controlled by the bit and bridle. God is the one who teaches and instructs us through His Word. So how can we spur one another on? By presenting and speaking the Word of God into each other's lives. The person who hears should respond with joy. But as we almost all have experienced, sometimes it takes a little spur to get someone moving. So we need to be that spur, stimulator, refresher, in people's lives.

And hopefully, through this, may we be reminded and see the truth that there is purpose and meaning to this life and theirs.

Chapter 4

WE HAVE A PURPOSE

Purpose—it is one of those big questions in life. Why am I here? What am I supposed to do? Is there something outside of me, past what I might be able to see, that is really driving me? What is my motivation for life? Why should I get out of bed in the morning, and what keeps me going when I don't feel like it?

We all ask these questions or these kind of questions. We all want to have a purpose. We want to know what is driving us. If we look honestly at our lives, I believe we could say we all want to be part of something bigger than just us. We want to have a purpose. We want to have meaning.

Purpose gives meaning to life. Without a purpose, we are back to being zombies or drifting through life. And even zombies could be argued to have purpose—they have to eat. In the same way, we all have a purpose we are following, even if we do not know it. Some of us are following our desires and are letting them give us meaning, and they have become our purpose in life. Others look to family and friends, looking to relationships to define them and give them meaning. Other people and how they view you and relate to you has become their purpose.

I worked a youth camp for a month, one summer. It was a blast, and I had a great time, but there was one problem. A friend had asked me to help run the sound for a program, and I was more than glad to help. This would have required me to do most of the tech stuff, the behind-the-scenes tasks. I was excited to help out this ministry and play a needed part. Imagine my dismay when I got to the camp and found out that they already had a full-time tech person. The month was still great, but there was a shadow now over my time there. That shadow was that I felt useless, as if I had no purpose being there. This lack of purpose took an otherwise great experience and dampened it.

When we have no purpose, our lives are dampened. We live under a shadow with the thought, "I was made for more than this." Sometimes we just have that feeling of being unfulfilled or lacking. We don't realize it is a lack of purpose until we dig a little and uncover that need we all have.

When you have a purpose, everything else in life falls under it. It is the organizing factor in your life. You wake up with that grand purpose in mind, and it leads you to do certain things and not to do others. For example, the person who sees family as her purpose will do whatever she needs to do to have that perfect family. All her tasks, even her job, are seen as a method of fulfilling that purpose. This also means that all her hopes and dreams are relying on how well her family performs.

Purpose has become very popular to talk about, with good reason. It is the directing element, the one thing that directs all else in our lives. We need only take a look at books like *The Purpose Driven Life* by Rick Warren. What Warren does is point to the truth that Christianity has been saying from the get-go: God gives us purpose. His purpose is better than any other and resounds throughout eternity.

If you follow Christ, you have purpose. Believe me, you do. Take a look at Romans 8:28, 29: "And we know that in all things God works for the good of those who love him, who have been called according to His purpose. For those God foreknew he also predestined to be conformed to the likeness of His son, that he might be the firstborn among many brothers."

This passage is part of one of my favorite passages in Scripture. It is pointing to the glorious truth of how God saves us and how God works in our lives. And in this great passage, we also see purpose.

God is working in our lives, and He has called us according to His purpose. Some people might say, "Well, that shows that God has a purpose in saving us, but that doesn't give us a purpose." God saved us and He called us because He has a purpose for us. It is in God's purpose that we find our purpose.

God has a purpose for everything He does, and that includes us. The amazing, life-changing truth about our faith is not that we are given a purpose, but that the Almighty God wraps us up in His purpose. Therefore what was His drive and purpose is now our purpose. God saved us for a reason, and it is that reason that should drive us.

We see more of that purpose in verse 29: we are to be conformed to the likeness of His Son. Part of our purpose is to be like Jesus, to be moving more and more toward looking like Christ. If this is our purpose, then we should organize our life on what makes us more like Christ, and then live accordingly. If this is our purpose, then it should be that directing element. That means we are guided and directed by what makes us fulfill this purpose. We head toward those activities, thoughts, and actions that make us conform to Christ, and we head away from those that don't.

Purpose is written throughout the Bible. We see it in the Old Testament, when God chooses a people to be the light on a hill, to draw in all other people to see Him. We see it in the New Testament, when God sends us out on a mission. Purpose has always been a part of how God has communicated with His people. Jeremiah 29:11 is probably the most famous verse about purpose. It points to the fact that God has a purpose for the nation of Israel and that they could trust in that. Why do people want to quote it to people all the time or write it on graduation notes? Because they want to reassure people who are at a crossroads in life or are questioning that they have a purpose.

Never doubt that you have a purpose. If you know God through Jesus Christ, you have a purpose, and that purpose is great. "Well, what is it?" you might be asking. The answer is simple: to live for Christ. All Christians have this purpose. How that purpose is played out and looks in your life is going to be a little different for each person. But the overarching purpose is the same. We are called to follow Christ, to live for Him, to become more and more like Him, and to make Him known.

It is not easy resting in this, it is not automatic, and it doesn't mean you can turn off your brain—but it does mean that you should have a drive, motivation, and reason for all you do. It means you should live intentionally.

God has a purpose for you . . . are you ready?

Chapter 5

GOD'S WILL

I sat across from her as she stated, with tears in her eyes, "I think I missed out on God's will for my life." She was expressing an all-too-common belief that somehow she was supposed to turn right and had ended up turning left and now she was "outside of God's will for her life." She knew—just knew—that she was supposed to have gone a different route, yet she took another one. She had been living with this feeling that she was in a second-tiered life, plan B, playing on the junior varsity team.

We want, we crave, and we need to know God's will for our lives. I have worked in youth ministry in many different capacities for many years, and I hear this all the time. Young people and older people alike all want to know what God wants them to do. They feel like they need divine revelation on a certain decision or path in life.

On the surface, this is God-honoring. On the surface, this looks like someone who is seeking to have God first in her life and seeking to have her whole life lived out for Christ. And most people who are asking this question are honestly motivated by a desire to please and live for God. But this attitude is really showing a lack of trust in, and a small view of, God.

This attitude stems from a belief that we can thwart God's plan for our lives. People who get hung up on looking for God's will for their lives usually are thinking that, if they don't make the right decision, there is a chance they will end up outside of God's will and will end up living some second-tier life of misery and gloom.

But that is not true. This is an imperfect way of looking at God's will. This is addressing what Kevin DeYoung calls God's will of direction, or the belief that God has a secret will of direction that He expects us to find out.[4] But I would argue that this is not how we should think of God's will. God doesn't send us on a scavenger hunt to find the plan He wishes us to follow.

Rather, the Bible speaks about God's will in two main categories. The first is God's will of decree, which is what will happen and does happen (one of the benefits of being the Almighty). The other idea is God's will of desire, which is what God wants us to do. This is where we find God's will for our lives. It is spelled out for us in the Bible, summed up in Jesus's command to follow.

God never expected us to try to find out His "will" for our lives like some treasure map to the blessed life He wants us all to have. We need to kill this view of God's will for our lives, because it leads to insecurity, uncertainty, doubt, depression, and anxiety. These are all things that God doesn't want for

---

4. Kevin DeYoung, *Just Do Something* (Chicago: Moody Publishers, 2009), 24.

us. If you don't believe me, take a look at Kevin DeYoung's Book *Just Do Something*. It is a great look at this topic, and he explains the position much better than I do and in greater detail.

God has blessed us incredibly with His Word. In it, we not only have the truth of who God is and how He loves us, we not only have the life-shattering gift of His Son sent to die for us, we not only have the eternal hope of being secure in His hands, but we also have instruction on how we are to respond. God has told us how to live. He has revealed how He desires us to respond to His love, grace, and mercy.

So what does God want from us? He wants us. He wants all of us. He wants all of who we are. We see this again and again throughout Scripture. We see Paul saying we should offer up our lives as living sacrifices to God; that all we are is owed Him. We have James telling us that we confirm and prove our faith by living for God, living our faith out in real and tangible ways. He specifically mentions taking care of people in need and doing good deeds. But these are broad commands, and many people want specifics. They want to know what God's will is for them, laid out in intricate detail.

Whenever this question comes up, I love pointing people to 1 Thessalonians:

It is God's will that you should be sanctified.
—1 Thess. 4:3

Be joyful always; pray continually; give thanks in all circumstances, for this is God's will for you in Christ Jesus.
—1 Thess. 5:16–18

In 1 Thessalonians 4, it tells us point-blank what God's will for our lives is: He wants us to be sanctified. So what does that mean? Sanctification is the process by which someone is made holy, set apart, more like Christ. To be sanctified is to be putting your faith into action and to be maturing in your Christian walk. This is a call to grow up, to become a person of maturity and start looking like your Lord, Jesus Christ. Whenever someone asks, "What is God's will for my life?" the answer is, "To look like Jesus." God wants you to be set apart for Him.

In 1 Thessalonians 5, Paul gives us a little bit more about how we can go about this. God wants us to be people who are joyful, praying, and giving thanks in what is coming our way. It really is that simple. We need joy, a lasting satisfaction in our Lord—a knowledge that we have all we need in Him and that He will provide. We need to be connected to God through prayer. We need to remind ourselves again and again that God has our backs and He is in control. And we need to thank Him for all we have, in all circumstances. That means, even on cruddy days, we thank God.

This is God's will for your life. It is that simple. He has it spelled out for us. But I am willing to bet that those who ask this question haven't put these simple actions into practice yet. If we put these actions into practice, I am willing to bet that much of our anxiety will go away. Why? Because we will be praying (Philip. 4:6, 7) and we will be joyful.

How would your life change if you really took that to heart? Those of us who struggle with the details of life and what God wants us to do have to be honest and say that life would change in drastic ways. Others haven't thought of it and need to be reminded that God wants you to live His way.

God wants you to live life for Him. In the mundane, in the sacred, in the everyday moments, in the big events, in everything and every second, God wants us to live for Him. That is why Paul says, in Colossians 3:23, to work at everything as if you are working for the Lord: because you are. In the midst of pain and suffering, live for God. In the midst of happiness and pleasure, live for God. In the midst of successes and failures, live for God. In all of life's ups and downs, live for God. That is God's will for your life.

Consider my favorite quote from Augustine of Hippo: "Love God and do whatever you please: for the soul trained in love to God will do nothing to offend the One who is Beloved."

Chapter 6

WE ARE ON A MISSION

I come from a family of boys. I have three older brothers, four nephews on my side of the family, and a son. My wife grew up with sisters and struggled to understand our son, who runs around, turning everything into a weapon and hitting anything and everything he can. When I hang out with my nephews, I can get them to do things they normally wouldn't want to, such as help out, by acting as if it is a special mission. When it's phrased that way, their whole attitude changes. Being sent on a mission is exciting, and it moves us to action.

I remember playing as a kid at my grandparents' cabin in Colorado. We, my brother or cousin and me, would routinely act like we were on a mission and try to sneak around. One of our favorites was making my grandpa stand on the deck and be on lookout for us as we tried to get up to him. Of course he easily spotted us, but it was still exciting. It was fun to act with a purpose and to have a destination and goal in mind. Being on a mission directs all you do and how you see life.

Why is being sent on a mission so powerful? Because it promises purpose and meaning. When we are on a mission, we know why we are doing what we are doing, because when you are on mission you don't engage in activities that interfere with the mission. Would you expect to see James Bond playing video games when he is supposed to be figuring out who is about to destroy the world? No, because he is on a mission. Would you expect Navy SEALs to take a detour to grab some beers while they are in the middle of infiltrating enemy territory? No, because they are on a mission.

When we are on mission, we have purpose and meaning to our life. We know what we are to do and why we are to do it. There is reason, a goal, and a way that you can reach the destination. This makes life fulfilling and exciting!

And God has a mission for us. God has a mission for you. And that mission is God's own mission.

How does that make you feel? When you read that God has a mission for you, what was your reaction? It should fill you with joy, a drive, and a reason for your existence. Just think about what this means—that the Almighty God is including you in His mission, that God wants you to be a part of what He is doing in the world. That is earth-shattering. God uses us to work in this world and carry out His mission. This should make us like little kids, who will do what they wouldn't normally do because being on a mission makes it fun.

So take a look inside. How does being on a mission from God make you feel? Because that will determine how well you are going to live intentionally for Him.

Maybe we need to have the attitude of the Blues Brothers. If you recall the movie, they get sent on a mission to get money for the orphanage they grew up in. Throughout the movie, they explain their actions and motivations with the simple line, "We are on a mission from God." And then they do everything in their power to fulfill that mission. We need to have, at a minimum, the same conviction.

So what is our mission? We see it throughout the Bible, and especially in the New Testament: We are sent by God to be His ambassadors and His representatives to a dark world. We are to love God and love others and share who Jesus is with the world. It is that simple—simply said, but a little harder to do.

We see the main thrust of this mission in the "Greats," The Great Commandment and the Great Commission. These two go together and work together. The Great Commandment is found in Matthew 22:37-40, in which Jesus says that the greatest commandment is to love the Lord your God with all your heart, soul, and mind, and that the second one is to love your neighbor as yourself. The Great Commission is also found in Matthew, in 28:18-20. Here Jesus gives His final command to his disciples: to make disciples of all nations, baptizing them and teaching them all they have learned from Jesus.

Both of these have been written about in length in many places. You can go very in-depth with each of them and find out all you could possibly want to know about what is implied and stated and meant. I recommend you do that if you are interested, and maybe even if you are not. But I am going to limit myself and draw out just a few things.

The Great Commandment gives us the foundation of the mission: love. This should not surprise us, since if you know God and Jesus, you know true love. Love is the foundation for following God. His very existence demands and requires it. It is like kissing my wife: I have to. It is not written into any contract or prenuptial agreement, but I have to. Why? Because when I am around her and see her and know what she means to me, that is something I just have to do. When we know God, loving Him is just something we have to do. This love drives us—it drives us to give our all to Him, to let Him guide and direct our lives. It also drives us to love others. We love others because we know love from God. That love from God trickles down into all of our relationships and interactions.

If you follow the Great Commandment, you are doing well. You have the right motivation and the right driving factor—love. But when you combine that with the Great Commission, you now have real purpose and meaning for your life, because the Great Commission now shows us in specifics how we are to live out this love. We love God, so we have to share Him! Have you ever gotten a present that you wanted so much and had been begging for? What did you do with it? You wanted everyone to see it and bask in its glory. That is kind of like what the Great Commission is saying. Yes, you know God, the Maker, the Creator, the Savior, and all the joyous excitement that brings, and now you get to share Him! You go and teach people about Him, baptizing them when they come to believe in Him, all through His authority and for His glory.

That is our mission. If you know Jesus Christ as your Savior, this is your mission. There are no outs, no buts, and no exceptions. You are on mission. Live like it.

Chapter 7

HELPLESS BUT NOT HOPELESS

Parents know what it means to be helpless. It comes when their child is sick, and they can't do anything to soothe or heal them. It comes when their child is independent and stubborn. We feel powerless in these situations.

This points to one of the fundamental aspects of human existence: you are helpless. At this, most of us want to rise up and declare, "Am not!" But it is a truth that the Bible makes very clear. We like to think of ourselves as strong and independent, but we are not. We are helpless because we suffer under the condition of sin and can't help but live enslaved to sin and rebellion against God. We are helpless because we can't free ourselves, save ourselves, or help ourselves. This is the truth declared in Romans 3:23: "For all have sinned and fall short of the glory of God." This is the point of Romans 6, where Paul talks about us being "slaves to sin." We are helpless.

It reminds me of my son, Titus, who is two-and-half years old. One day, he was running around the church as my wife was preparing for a children's event. He found a balloon and proceeded to try to blow this balloon up by himself. He slobbered all over the poor balloon, blowing spit everywhere. He was helpless. Because his lips weren't making a good seal, all the air he blew was going out the sides. Even if he could get a good seal, his lungs weren't strong enough to blow up the balloon. And after a moment, like most kids, he lost interest and moved on.

Like my son unable to blow up the balloon, on our own, we can't live for God and do what He requires. We will fail every single time. We don't know how, even with the Bible's clear direction and commands. We have lived counter-God for so long that all of our behavior and habits are based on sin, not God. We don't have the strength to not fail, to not sin. We don't have the energy to follow and the willpower to always make the right choices.

We are helpless without Christ—but never hopeless.

We have hope, a hope not found in ourselves, but rather in our God and in our Savior Jesus Christ. We see this when we finish the sentence started in Romans 3:23, which concludes in verse 24 with this: "and are justified freely by his grace through the redemption that came by Jesus Christ." We have hope not in our righteousness, deeds, skills, or talents, but rather in our Savior. We have hope because we have received redemption through God's grace that comes through Jesus Christ. Your abilities are not mentioned because they do not matter for your salvation. Our hope comes from God, and Him alone, because He saved us in Christ alone, through faith alone, by grace alone, to His glory alone.

What does this have to do with living an intentional life? Everything. If we try to live a life that is intentionally pointing to God in everything we do, but we do it on our own or by ourselves, we are helpless, doomed to failure. But we do this all the time.

I once saw a man driving down the road with a mattress loosely tied to the top of his car. The mattress appeared ready to fall off, but the man was confidently holding it with one arm hooked out the window. Physics tells us this is a bad idea, but humans often think of themselves as superheroes. Just surf the internet for a little bit and you'll find video after video of people thinking they can do anything—and ending up in the hospital. And we bring this mindset into our faith. It doesn't matter how often we have failed before, we somehow think that this time will be different. Paul says in Galatians 3:3, "Are you so foolish? After beginning with the Spirit are you now trying to attain your goal by human effort?" And the answer is yes. We are indeed that foolish. God saves us through Jesus, and He also empowers us to live through Jesus.

To live an intentional life, we first have to admit that we are helpless on our own. We admit that we can't do this on our own. We are not smart enough, intelligent enough, funny enough, hardworking enough, or anything that would enable us to live for God and to live intentionally. When we admit that, we are freed because we will know that our success depends on the One who is working within us. We are freed from thinking that our worth relies on our skills and talents rather than on who God made us to be.

It is the same thought behind Jesus's seemingly confusing statement in Luke 9:24: "Whoever wants to save his life will lose it, but whoever loses his life for me will save it." When we realize that living empowered and directed by God and walking with Jesus throughout all of our life, when we are constantly taking ourselves off the thrones of our lives so that Jesus can have His rightful place, then we will have life. Give all your life to Jesus to have life.

Chapter 8

WATCH YOUR LIFE

I am a nerd. Books were my friends when I was growing up, and I still run to them whenever I am down or have a spare moment. My parents joke that I had the perfect excuse for getting out of chores around the house: if they asked me to do something when I was reading, I'd act as if I didn't hear them. When faced with which child to assign a chore—the kid who was reading or the kid watching TV—they often chose the kid watching TV. My brothers are still mad about it.

This love for reading translates to my Christian life. My dad gave me two books when I went off to college, *Knowledge of the Holy* by A.W. Tozer and *Knowing God* by J.I. Packer. These books changed the course of my life. I was already in love with God, but now I was in love in understanding my faith and learning godly ideas.

I watch my doctrine closely. In fact, I watch most people's doctrine very closely. At some of the lower moments in my life, I would describe myself to be a doctrine watchdog. I would examine sermons under a theological microscope, looking for any variations from what I perceived to be the truth. There is some good to this: we should watch what we believe, what we teach, and what others teach, and we need to be on guard against any untruth we see or hear.

However, the problem comes in when people like me, who are concerned with theology, keep our noses in books and really only care about a well-organized and theologically accurate position. This is a danger that we must be aware of, just as Paul says: "Knowledge puffs up, but love builds up" (1 Cor. 8:1).

Watch your life and doctrine closely. Persevere in them, because if you do, you will save both yourself and your hearers.

—1 Tim. 4:16

We are not only supposed to watch what we believe (our doctrine), but we are supposed to watch our lives as well. These two go together more than we sometimes think. Doctrine influences and directs our lives. Our lives reflect and reveal what we believe about God, ourselves, and the world. No matter how much some want to separate them, you can't. They are intrinsically connected.

So what is "watching your life"? Your life is all of who you are. The whole of your existence can be described as your life. This means that all of your thoughts, actions, interactions, and relationships are part of your life. These are what we need to watch. Why are we watching them? To see if they align with the Word of God.

I hate getting my tires aligned. I don't like spending money on a problem I can't really see. Why can't I see the problem of my tires being out of alignment? Because you need tools and a computer to tell you your tires are out of whack. So how do

I know if my life is out of whack? The answer is the Word of God, which cuts through all of our pretenses and delusions to reveal what God expects of us.

We are commanded to watch our multifaceted lives and our doctrine closely. Our doctrine is what we believe about God, humanity, and this existence. We must continuously filter and examine all of what we believe. And the filter is the Word of God. In this new life in Christ, we must always take every thought and every belief back to the Bible. If it doesn't line up with what we know, it has to be questioned. This is why Paul talks about "being renewed in knowledge" (Col. 3:10) and "transformed by the renewing of your mind" (Rom. 12:2).

We have a great promise if we are watchful. We can be assured that we have salvation, and not just for ourselves, but also for those we teach. We can be assured that what we believe and how we are living is matching the will of God for our lives. And when we are aligned with God's will, our relationship with Jesus is on track, and no doubts hinder us.

So how do we watch closely? By living intentionally, having a purpose that drives us and a meaning that guides us. Waking up every day knowing that what we do has a reason requires that we watch what we do. To know that every belief we have will influence our actions (which in turn have purpose) requires that we watch our doctrine. Watch yourself to make sure that you are living out your life as you are commanded. Make sure that you align with God. Moment-by-moment, walk with God.

What would this look like? Maybe start by examining actions and asking why you are doing them. If they do not bring glory to God, then they are diverging you from your purpose. Then intentionally change them so that they reflect your purpose. Maybe capture thoughts and put them under the microscope of Scripture to see if they are true or not. These are general ideas, but let's get specific.

I used to like to watch a show on TV that I knew was not really glorifying to God. It had violence and sexual elements and other aspects that it was putting into my mind. I justified watching it, but it was just that, a justification for my desires. It took my wife's encouraging me (forcefully) to look at this in light of Christ and my faith in Him. I had to take a look at my life and what was in this show; watching it was out of alignment with His Word. What was the solution? I stopped. I didn't like stopping, and it took my wife's being my conscience, but I did it. It might not seem like such a big deal, but I know that my life is more closely aligned with God than it was before.

I challenge you to take a look and then take a step. Little-by-little, you can watch your life and doctrines closely by living intentionally.

Chapter 9

FLEE AND PURSUE

But you, man of God, flee from all this, and pursue righteousness, godliness, faith, love, endurance and gentleness.

—1 Tim. 6:11

There is a story of the Korean War, where, during the Battle of Chosen Reservoir, the commanding officer of the First Marine Division, Oliver Smith, made the famous remark, "Retreat, hell! We're not retreating, we're just advancing in a different direction."[5] The marines were surrounded and were withdrawing. To do this they had to fight their way to their destination.

In living intentionally, we have to do this same thing. We have to withdraw from some things, but we are surrounded

---

5. http://www.vincehuston.org/quotes/marines_chosin.html.

and have to be willing to fight to get to our destination. Intentional living is not always easy, and it might just require us to go to battle.

Paul tells Timothy to flee from all of this. So what must Timothy and we flee from? When we look at the context, we see that we are to withdraw from any false doctrine, any wayward beliefs. We are to have nothing to do with people who teach ideas, concepts, or philosophies that lead people astray. Does this mean that we can't prepare our minds and go to combat to take captive these strongholds of deceptive philosophy? No, but it does mean that we guard our minds from false thoughts and filter our thoughts by the truth of God's Word. It means that we are ready to direct others to the truth and point out the faults in these ideas. And it means that we watch who teaches in our churches, making sure that we are not led astray.

We are also supposed to flee from the oh-so-subtle lure of money and desiring it. I know that this can be subtle, and have struggled with it myself. It eases its way into our thinking so that, before we know it, we're viewing security as coming from our bank account. We might have the best of motives at the start—taking care of family, or something like that—but those motives can change all too quickly. We are to flee from the love of money because it wrestles for our attention and devotion. We must flee from anything that takes our eyes off of Christ.

And we don't just flee, we turn our focus and our minds in another direction. We turn from that which is not Christ-honoring and Christ-focused and turn to those things that are. So what are we to turn to?

We are called to pursue certain things. When I read about pursuing, I think of a chase. We are called to pursue. That means we chase down what is from God. Is there anything more intentional than chasing down something? You become driven to catch it, to use everything in your power to run it down. This is living with intent; you are intent in all your actions so that you can literally tackle the qualities of God to the ground.

We are to pursue righteousness. This includes living in alignment with God's Word, but also more. We pursue righteousness by pursuing a relationship with Christ, who first pursued us. It is not our effort that enables us to be in right standing before God and to live according to His Word; only through Christ can we gain that standing.

Godliness is being like God, having those qualities that God has. There is only one way that we can know God well enough to imitate Him, and that is by knowing Him through His self-revelation. We study the Bible so that we can know our God, our Lord and our Savior.

One quality we must pursue is faith. Many people think faith is something a person just has or hasn't got. But have you ever considered that faith is something to be pursued and sought after rather than a have or have-not? The disciples asked Jesus to increase their faith. We know that faith is a gift from God. Faith needs to be practiced and sought just as other qualities of the Christian life. Paul talks of Abraham being "strengthened in his faith" (Rom. 4:20, 21). When we put our faith into practice, it can grow. We need to be a people that seeks and runs after faith.

Love is one of the distinguishing marks of a Christian that we must pursue. Jesus says that by loving one another, we show others that we are following Him. That is a big deal. We want people to look at us and see Jesus in our actions and in our interactions. If they do not, that can mean trouble for our relationship with our Lord. Paul says that without love we are nothing, no matter what else we bring to the table. So do you want to be something? Do you want to reflect Jesus? Pursue love.

Living intentionally is a marathon, not a sprint. It is about the totality of our life, not just one or two quick moments. For this reason, we need to pursue the discipline of endurance, the ability to endure. We need to be a people that can keep on keeping on. Just like building physical endurance, we need to build spiritual endurance.

The last quality that Paul listed for Timothy to pursue is gentleness. I find it funny that this is listed for someone whom Paul has to encourage later, "God has not given us a spirit of timidity, but a spirit of power of love and of self-discipline" (2 Tim. 1:7). But gentleness is to be kept in mind because how we treat others matters. How we use the incredible power of Christ inside us matters. We take Jesus as a model: He who was the Almighty in the flesh was also gentle in how He interacted with others. We have the truth, but it must be spoken in love. We have salvation, so we must be thoughtful of others who do not. Pursuing gentleness helps keep others in our minds.

Many people think of the faith as a list of what not to do. And the idea of fleeing from certain things can encourage that conception of Christianity. They see limits and restriction. But we need to have the same attitude as the proud Marine, to whom retreat went against everything in him. It wasn't a retreat; he was just attacking in a different direction, the direction in which he and his company wanted to go. Why focus on the fleeing? To focus on the things that have lasting meaning and value. When we go toward what truly matters, we pursue that which is worthwhile eternally and gives meaning to life.

Chapter 10

FIGHT THE GOOD FIGHT

Fight the good fight of the faith. Take hold of the eternal life to which you were called when you made your confession in the presence of witnesses.
                                        —1 Tim. 6:12

Ever have a friend who was just looking for a fight? I have. It's uncomfortable to have to watch them and make sure they are not going to drag you into bad situations. It makes being with them a chore, having to be on your guard all the time. The fact of the matter is that many people are looking for a fight. They are looking for that challenge, that struggle, or that something to give them purpose.

People have used this as one of those common traits of men—that we are all looking to be a part of that great battle. And I think that is generally true. But I also think that it goes beyond men—all humans are looking for something bigger than themselves to fight for. This means that millions of people are looking for a fight, a cause to take up, the contest to define them, and the meaning it brings.

God has given us a purpose. When we realize that, we start to see that we are to fight the good fight. This is, in fact, good. Fighting to follow God, fighting for intentionality in all your actions and thoughts—these are good. It is what we were designed for and the purpose behind who we are. We were made for this.

It is the struggle between what we were and who we are now. We have the battle raging within ourselves. The past habits and desires are fighting against our new life in Christ. This battle will end in our favor, because Christ will bring what He started to completion. But while it rages, we fight.

This battle flows out of us and impacts all those around us. When we are winning the battle and are triumphing over the desires of the flesh, our life seems more on track. Our relationships are generally better, we are nicer, we have others in mind more, and we are not seeking those things that are destroying us. When we have suffered some defeat, fallen to a temptation, our relationships can feel the blunt of frustration and anger. This inward battle starts to affect all of our lives and all of those around us.

It is also an outside battle. We have to fight to live out our faith. We have to destroy those ways of living that are not of the faith and start new ways that glorify God. Once again, this is not easy. Battles are not easy. It is not easy because it is a fight, and our old ways fight back. And sometimes they fight back hard. The ways of comfort and routine and what is easy fight against new ways that are unfamiliar and might make us stretch and put ourselves "out there" more. But it is a worthwhile fight, because a life lived outwardly for God impacts all those around us. It can be an effective apologetic tool as well as a great way to build friendships and show people you care about them.

This fight, inside and out, is a fight to be what God wants you to be. In that aspect, it is a fight worth doing and doing to the utmost. God has laid out what He wants for us, and now we fight for it. We fight to be worthy of this calling. We fight to be worthy of this love. We fight for Him in all areas of our lives. While we cannot earn or make ourselves good enough in His eyes (that only comes through Christ), we fight to give our lives as living sacrifices for Him. We fight in response to what He has done. God has given us life, He has given us purpose, and He has given us meaning and direction. So we fight the good fight in response to our Savior. J.C. Ryle puts it like this: "The believer is a soldier. There is no holiness without warfare. Saved souls will always be found to have fought a fight."[6]

Are you ready to fight? If not, you'd better start training.

I love how this verse ends. We are commanded to take hold of the eternal life that we are called to. This eternal life is not something that awaits us when we die. It starts when we come to know Christ. Our eternal life includes this right now. If you know Christ as your Lord and Savior, then as you read this your eternal life has already begun. Yes, you still have a distance to go. You still will be sanctified more and more because the final glorification is yet to come. But we are commanded to take hold of the hope, the promise, and the glory now!

This means that we are to realize not only how God made us, but to realize what that new life in Christ means. We are to grasp who we are in Christ. The fact that God considers us His children, that He loves us like Christ, that He sees us as

---

6. J.C. Ryle, *Holiness* (East Peoria, IL: Versa Press, 2014), 77.

co-heirs alongside Christ should get our hearts pumping. It should get us out of our seats and make us want to live a life worthy of our Lord. Realize who you are! And then live like it!

What would happen if we did that? We would start to live intentionally. We would see purpose and meaning in all that we did. If we didn't see that purpose, we would examine what we did through the lens of Christ and seek to do everything for Him. In our work, home, friendships, hobbies, and every single moment we would keep Christ at the forefronts of our minds and seek to magnify His glory.

Every moment would start to drip with meaning and purpose.

Every day would become a worship song sung by our actions and our thoughts as we sought to live for the glory of God, our Father.

Are you ready for that? Do you want it? Then fight for it!

Chapter 11

A LIFE WORTHY

Whatever happens, conduct yourselves in a manner worthy of the gospel of Christ.

—Philip. 1:27a

"He made me so mad!" "She made me do it!" "Life is just so busy right now." "I'll get back on track when life calms down."

Do any of these sound familiar? We are great at blaming our actions on our circumstances or on other people's actions.

Think back to when you were a kid. I am willing to bet that you used the excuse "She/He made me do it!" or "They made me so mad!" As kids, we often believed that someone else had pushed us into a corner, so to speak, and forced our actions a bit, but that excuse never held up under the scrutiny of Mom and Dad. Mom and Dad knew the truth: that we are all responsible for our actions. We can't blame others for them.

But we still try these excuses today. If you have ever seen a marriage in trouble, you most likely have seen people blaming what they are doing on others—not always, but many times it is happening. If you have talked with someone about their spiritual disciplines, they more often than not use excuses about the circumstances of their life. People use the busyness and harshness of life to justify why they might not be reading their Bibles, not praying as they should, or not doing any number of things.

But Paul, in Philippians, tells us, "Whatever happens"— meaning that we can no longer use circumstances as an excuse for not living for, and living out, the gospel. The word *whatever* covers all contingencies and all possibilities. It doesn't leave room for any excuse. In our deepest grief, we need to live worthily of the gospel, and in our highest joy, we need to live for the gospel.

The gospel of Christ becomes, according to Paul, our directing element and organizing factor. That means that it is the gospel that now determines what we should do and what we should not do. The gospel is in charge. To live a life worthy of the gospel means we have to live up to it, we have to live it out, we have to know it and breathe it and share it. So now, in all our actions, we have the filter of the gospel. Does this align or not? Is this part of the gospel or not?

Think through your life and your recent actions. See if they align with the gospel. If so, give thanks to God and keep on keeping on. If not, take some time and see how using the gospel as the directing element and organizing factor would change each action, situation, interaction, and thought.

To have the gospel as that which we organize our life around and that which we allow to direct us, we need to know it. And not just know it cognitively or intellectually, but also to match that knowledge with experience. We need to know it personally and to live it out personally.

The gospel of Christ, the good news of the anointed one, is

that Christ came to save sinners, even a wretch like me. That is the good news. Romans 5:8 rings out with this truth: "But God demonstrates his own love for us in this, while we were still sinners Christ died for us." We need to hold onto this truth, that we are saved by the grace of God, by the blood of Christ, for the glory of God. That is the base of the good news.

We are saved, and we must act like it. So, we say, saved from what? Saved from sin, the condition that was keeping us from God, the condition that was leading to those individual sins that harm people and ourselves. We were pulled out of that, so we should not live like we used to live anymore. We should discard that former life and live like those who have been saved for something better. This is the sentiment of 1 Corinthians 6:9–11. People who are characterized by sin are not following the gospel. But there is hope, because we have all come out of that way of life. Now we need to live like people who are saved.

When we come to know the gospel, we understand that we are no longer our own. In our day and age, this rubs so many people the wrong way. One of the highest values the culture promotes is to be in charge of your own life and be your own boss. We crave our independence so much that to think that we are not our own gets people mad. But that is the gospel truth and it is glorious! 1 Corinthians 6:19 reminds us of this great truth. God has bought us. We who believe have been purchased by the death of Christ—we are no longer our own. This means that we should live like we are God's. I call this great news because God takes responsibility for us. We are no longer on our own; God has given us everything we need to live like one of His. He has given us His Holy Spirit, so we are empowered to live out this life of faith. He has given us His Word, so that we can understand how we are to respond to Him and how much He loves us. He has given us His Body, the church, so that we can be in a community that cares for each other and lifts one another up. What else do we need? Nothing.

The gospel directs us, and the gospel organizes our lives. It gives us purpose and meaning. The gospel tells us the truth of what God has done for us and what we are called to do in response. It is our motivation for life and for a life lived well. And now we are to live it out.

Live worthy, my friends.

Chapter 12

LIVE INTENTIONALLY

Living intentionally—that is the goal of living out our faith. It is a call for all of us who believe in Jesus as our Lord and Savior to live with purpose and meaning. This is found throughout the Bible and is a mandate that we should all run toward. It has benefits that far outweigh the costs, so why don't we do it? It goes against our nature, at least our sinful nature. It is work and it requires thought, both of which the enemy doesn't want us to get used to employing. But God calls us to do it.

Living intentionally looks daunting when you think about your whole life and making every aspect align with Scripture. But think about what happens when you start thinking about it moment-by-moment. It is living life as it comes, but not without a plan or thinking through it. It is processing life by moments so that, at any moment, we can stop and think through whether that moment was aligned with God's Word and used for God's glory. It doesn't matter what that moment was—a thought, an action, what you are taking in, or what you are putting out there. They are all moments and looking at them individually might help us from seeing this task as daunting.

It would be our hope that as we put this practice of living intentionally into action that the moments which reflect God would increase and those that do not would decrease. Because life is a collection of those moments we have, what you make of those moments is what your life ends up being. By watching the moments and making them what you want, your life will follow suit and be an intentionally lived life. Just as changing a system or the world so often starts with one person, so changing a life starts by changing one moment and then the next and then the next.

Living intentionally sounds hard—and like something we would fail at doing. And we do not like failure. No one has ever liked it, but it seems that this fear of failure has become more and more restricting than before. People now won't do new things or take chances because they are afraid they will fail. It cripples us, makes us stunted.

I think this fear comes from associating who we are with what we do and what we achieve. So now failing means that we are failures. It means that we will always carry that around with us and never be successful. This is a lie from the enemy. I have seen it worm its way into my own life, and it is destructive. I failed. I was fired from being a pastor. Not just any pastoral job, but my dream pastoral job (at that time). It killed me. My life was shattered. Why? Because I viewed myself as a failure.

Who you are is determined not by what you do or have done, but rather by whom you know. Understanding that changes lives. Your identity is found in Christ as a son or daughter of God—nowhere else. Hold that firmly to your chest and never let it go. When advertisements or friends or the enemy try to whisper into your ear that you are defined by anything else, whip this out and declare the truth. Never forget it, because knowing this allows you to take chances because you no longer fear failing.

The fear of failing at living intentionally can also be conquered in understanding that living is moment-by-moment. If we fail one moment, it is just a moment and not the end of the world. Each moment can be a failure to learn from or a victory to add to our ever-growing mound of victories. And then, by the grace of God (because God empowers us to live out our faith), we can look back on our victories and see a life that had purpose and meaning.

Each moment is an opportunity to live out our faith, impact those around us, and live for God. Every moment. Think about that. Each moment, you have a chance, the ability, the freedom, the power, and the mandate to live for God and have your faith spill out on those around you. What a great life we live! Maybe, just maybe, this is what Jesus meant when He said that He gives us life abundant. Can you imagine a fuller life than one lived moment-by-moment for God? I can't.

So I challenge and encourage you to do this. Live intentionally. Find a way to check yourself moment-by-moment to make sure you are on track. Paul commands this in 2 Corinthians 13:5. Grab a partner and do it together. Grab your spouse and do married life intentionally. You will not regret it.

Because it is either living with a purpose or being a zombie, and that is not living at all.

Chapter 13

THE LIFE OF A DISCIPLE

Are you a disciple? The answer is yes, in case you were wondering. A disciple is a person who follows another person's teaching and spreads it to others. We all follow something or someone, so we are all disciples. If you believe in Jesus Christ, then you are His disciple, because to believe in Him is to follow Him.

There are some who think that being a disciple is a second step or the "next level" in their walk with Jesus. And I will agree that being aware of following and actively pursuing Jesus will come with maturity. But all believers are called to be disciples, and all believers are disciples. We just might not be the best disciples yet. We need to grow in what it means to be a disciple.

So where would you rate yourself on this? Are you actively living as a disciple?

When we read the gospel of Luke, it becomes clear that this is a radical calling. It is one that changes your life and demands your all. Just take a look at Luke 9:23: "Then he said to them all: 'If anyone would come after me, he must deny himself and take up his cross daily and follow me.'" This verse shows that to be a disciple means to live intentionally for Christ.

Jesus starts off with, "If anyone would come after me." Other translations have Him saying, "If anyone would be my disciple." So this verse is telling us the requirements of being a disciple. Discipleship starts with three commands: deny, take, and follow. These are actions that are part of what it means to be a disciple. Following commands requires effort and intentionality, which means that we have to choose to follow. We have to make a choice: whether we are going to be disciples as Christ defines them.

We are called to deny ourselves, to put Christ's ways before our ways, to lay down our life for others, to not think we are the center of the world, to be ready to serve Christ and others even when it interferes with what we have planned. Darrell Johnson says that to deny yourself means "to deny your self-lordship. It means saying no to the god who is me, to reject the demands of the god who is me, to refuse to obey the claims of the god who is me."[7] This might be the hardest thing for us to do, because it requires a constant killing of pride and our ego. We have to continually and intentionally put to death the belief that we are our own masters and rulers and kings. Do you deny yourself for Christ?

We are called to take up our cross. This can be confusing because we it sounds as if we must endure hardship. But Jesus means for us to realize that following Him means counting ourselves dead to all else. A person's picking up the cross to be crucified meant that his life was over. There was no way out,

7. Darrell Johnson, quoted in Greg Oden, *Discipleship Essentials*, 28.

and they were as good as dead. So when Jesus commands us to do this, He is saying that our former lives are over. Darrell Johnson says it this way: "Jesus calls his followers to think of themselves as already dead, to bury all our earthly hopes and dreams, to bury the plans and agendas we made for ourselves. He will either resurrect our dreams or replace them with dreams and plans of his own."[8] To be a disciple means submitting our whole life to our Lord. Are you taking up your cross?

We are called to do this daily. It is on a regular basis that we have to make this choice, to take up the cross or not, to deny ourselves or not, to follow or not. It is in this regular pattern that we find intentionality, for if we do not plan to take up the cross on a daily basis, we most likely won't. It is much easier to live for ourselves than our Lord. It is easier to keep the control we think we have. It is more comfortable to follow our own dreams and plans than to trust God's. It is only when we are intentional about how we live that we can step into deeper discipleship and live out this verse.

And last, we are commanded to follow. Look to Jesus and follow Him. Where He leads, we go. It is as simple as that. To follow means we are intentionally looking and taking directions from our leader. To follow means that we are purposefully not doing some things and purposefully doing others. There can be no following without intentional behavior. So how well are you following?

Let's grow together in Christ as intentional disciples.

---

8. Ibid., 29.

Chapter 14

THE WORK

Work it out!

Jesus saves us. God gives us faith. Salvation from beginning to end is from God, but we are called to live and work it out. And that is where most of us struggle. We struggle in the daily grind. We struggle in applying what Christ has done for us to every part of our lives. We trust that God has made us new creations, and we know that God has given us new hearts, but the struggle is real.

You have felt that struggle. Someone cuts you off in traffic and your first response is to yell and contemplate their downfall (okay, maybe you won't go quite that far). Your spouse says something and you immediately take it the wrong way. Your kid spills milk, and you erupt. A co-worker gets the promotion you wanted and thought you deserved, so you covet and sulk. You know that looking at that person with those lustful thoughts is wrong, but it feels right in the moment. When hanging around friends, you give into the temptation to embellish and exaggerate, wanting to make more of your life. The list could go on. I bet you could think of many more examples from your life that show this struggle. We all have them. This is the real, everyday struggle of the Christian.

Philippians 2:12, 13 declares, "Continue to work out your salvation with fear and trembling, for it is God who works in you to will and to act according to his good purpose." It is in these verses that I think we see how we are supposed to respond to this struggle. And the answer is that we work, not from our own power, but from God's.

"Work out your salvation" is the call to put into action what we believe. There are several different ways we can view this phrase "work out." Think of it as a baker kneading dough to "work" all the ingredients into the whole loaf. This is the purposeful movement of all the ingredients to every part of the whole piece of dough. So we are called to push and pull and intentionally make sure that what we believe is present in all that we are. So "work out your salvation" can be seen as making sure that in all your life you are living, thinking, acting, and loving as one who has been saved.

You can also think of this phrase in terms of a classroom. When a student is given a question or a problem to solve, he might struggle. But what does a good teacher do? She might encourage the student by using a phrase such as "work it out." This is the encouragement not to give up, but rather to think it through. What would be the next step in solving the problem? What kind of operation or procedure is needed? In terms of our faith, we can see this as stopping and thinking through what we believe and how we are called to live as Christians. Think through and process what it means to be saved and what is demanded and required of you. What is the next step in your faith? How can you follow your Lord?

The final way that I see this phrase is in terms of physically working out. When we go to the gym, what do we do? We strain our muscles and put them through the paces. We purposely exercise so that we will be stronger. We intentionally do moves that will help build up our bodies. When we come at our faith from that angle, we can say that working out our salvation involves doing the intentional actions of our faith, no matter the strain, so that we will be built up in the ways of our Lord.

We should do this working with fear and trembling. There is indeed an element of being frightened, but the idea is having reverence for our God, knowing who saved us and what He has saved us from.

God has saved us from sin, our cosmic treason, as R.C. Sproul puts it. This is the heinous rebellion of ungrateful humans against their holy, just, perfect King. Knowing not only "the Who" that saves us, but also "the from what" we have been saved instills in us a sense of reverence and awe. We are amazed at the graciousness and love of God and therefore fall down before Him. We tremble because we know how great, immense, powerful, and perfect our God is. We fear, or give Him reverence, because we know that He didn't have to save us, but He chose to save us. The response that is appropriate is one of reverence and awe.

So we know what we are supposed to do when we struggle to live out our faith, but the question is, "How can we do this?" Once again, Paul speaks it clearly in Philippians 2:13. We can only do this because God is working in us. The "how" is "through the power of God working in us." This means that we can only work out our salvation because God is working in us. This is the truth found throughout Scripture. God not only saves us, but He also gives us the power to live out our salvation as well. And we also know that God brings it to completion, as Philippians 1:6 tell us: "And I am sure of this, that he who began a good work in you will bring it to completion at the day of Jesus Christ." God saves us, gives us the power to grow in His ways, and brings us to the end. Salvation is, from start to finish, a work of God.

But we don't think that way. This is why Paul said, in Galatians 3:3, "Are you so foolish? After beginning with the Spirit, are you now trying to attain your goal by human effort?" We *are* that foolish. God saves us not because of anything righteous we have done, but because of His mercy (Tit. 3:5). This is an act of the Spirit working in our hearts so that we are changed and choose to follow God. This Spirit makes us a new creation (2 Cor. 5:17). And after knowing this great and amazing fact—that God saves us—we then turn around and think, "I have to pull myself up by my bootstraps." What fools we are! Do we think that God, after saving us, will leave us to our own devices and our own power? Of course not! He continues to work in us so that we have all we need to live for Him. As 2 Peter 1:3 tells us, we have all we need for life and godliness. We have all we need to live for Him.

And this work that God is doing so that we can work out our salvation is twofold. God works on our wills. When we are regenerated by the Spirit, we are given a new will—a will that is aligned with God's will. One of the ways that God gives us power to follow Him is to help us will to follow and work out our salvation. This means that God helps us have the desire to follow Him. There is a battle going on before any action takes place, and that is the battle for our desires. God is working on us so that our desires match His desires. When our desires are on track, then the second way that God works in us naturally follows. God then works so that we have the power for our actions to align with His good purpose. These actions that follow God's purpose naturally flow from a will that has been captured by God. But even then, we need His help to continue to live for Him.

So how do we combat this struggle of living out our faith? We know the what—to work out our salvation. And we know the how—through God's power and not our own strength. And we should also know the why—for the good purpose of God. What is God's good purpose? It is to save you, grow you, and use you to bring others to know Him, ultimately for His glory. God's good purpose is that through His church, missions, and individual Christians, His name is glorified. If this is God's purpose, He won't let you down. He will make this happen, working in you so that you can work out your salvation.

Chapter 15

I.N.T.E.N.T.

When we are thinking about living intentionally, or with purpose, or however you want to say it, it can be helpful to have some tools or guidelines. These can be of different sorts. Some might help you think through how to have a life lived on purpose, and others might help you organize your day so that you can make the most out of it. Here is a tool that can help us to live with purpose every day. It comes in the acronym "I.N.T.E.N.T." This is just a simple way of remembering some key principles that can help us as we think about how to live with intentionality in all we do.

I decide to be Intentional with my life.
Not every intention is good.
Test intentions and plans against Scripture.
Expect opposition.
Never give up.
Tenacity is key.

I decide to be intentional with my life. This way of life, which I believe all Christians are called to, is a decision. It doesn't just happen. Each and every one of us has to decide that we are fed up with the status quo and desire more. We have to decide that we will follow. We decide to put our Lord's demands before our wants and desires. We decide to be intentional.

This decision is an ongoing process for life. This is not just one moment in time. Some people might become frustrated that they are not living intentionally and then decide at that moment to change. But if they don't continue to keep deciding and keep living out that decision, the moment will quickly fade away and they will be back where they started. Life is made up of a series of moments, and each of these moments has to be a decision to follow Jesus.

I live in the Bible belt. While some people might not like this term, it is accurate. People in my town are surrounded by churches, and most have at least some connection to a church. Because of this "cultural Christianity," there are many people who are trusting in that one moment or one decision for their whole life. They haven't grasped that life is a collection of moments and we need to be intentional in all of them.

This also means that no one can make this decision for you. You have to make it. You have to carry it out. It is a personal decision. Just as your initial decision to follow and believe in Jesus was a personal one that no one could do for you, so it is with the decision to continue and constantly follow. This is not your parents' decision, nor your spouse's decision, nor your church leader's decision. It is your decision. So what will you decide?

Not every intention is good. We need to recognize that we sometimes make plans that only benefit us. We act without considering the Lord. This is the warning in James chapter 4. We need, rather, to consider God and His will. We need to recognize that we still struggle with sin. And because of that struggle, we can very easily convince ourselves that our plans are the best, even when they are not. It is amazing how easy it is to justify almost anything. So we need to realize that not all our plans and intentions come from the purest of motives. You intend to get that promotion. Sounds good—and you can justify the extra hours away from home and time lost in which you could lead your family. But is that a good intention? Many would not hesitate—they would jump into that decision with both feet. But we are called to a higher standard, and that means realizing that some of our plans might not be good after all.

This is easy to see when we get hurt or are angry. When my son gets upset, he acts out, usually by trying to take a swing at me. He makes plans to strike back. Yes, they are usually in the moment, but it is a moment when he has an intent to hurt someone else because he is hurt. And, if we were honest, all too often we act the same way.

Test intentions and plans against Scripture. If we know that we can have bad intentions or plans, what do we do? We check all of them against Scripture. We seek to test all of what we intend with Scripture. If we believe that all Scripture is indeed God-breathed, then it makes sense that this should be our ultimate source for guidance and direction.

My wife and I recently bought a house, a much-needed upgrade from what we were living in. Before we moved in, we wanted to paint some rooms and do some light cosmetic housework. As I was painting our new dining room, I notice that the cold-air return had been painted over. Looking into the vent, I noticed that something seemed to be blocking it. There was an old filter, covered in at least an inch of dust and painted to the vent. Needless to say, that filter wasn't doing what it was designed to do.

Scripture is a filter for our decisions. And if we don't tend to our knowledge and understanding of Scripture, it can easily become like that clogged and painted-over filter. We need to be in Scripture and know it so that it will be a true and good filter. What does a good filter do? It lets the good pass and collects the bad. So Scripture can let the good decisions and intentions pass through while weeding out the bad.

Scripture also acts as an anchor (Heb. 6:19). It grounds us in what is important and what is true. It won't let us get off-track and follow the desires that are purely of the flesh. And we need this. Because without that anchor, we will find ourselves making decisions that are based solely on what we want, with no consideration for others or God.

Expect opposition. Living the way of the Lord goes against the ways of the world. The world says to do what you want, follow your heart, and you are the captain of your own fate. So when you decide to follow God rather than the ways of the world, you can expect that others will question you and make fun of you. They will look upon you as weird and strange. And that is to be expected. In fact, Peter tells us that strangers is really what we are. We are no longer like everyone else in this world, but rather we have new identities that call for a different way of life.

We should also expect opposition from ourselves. Even after making a decision to follow and being intentional, we can still face opposition from ourselves. This is because this way of life is foreign to us. It is an uphill battle that takes effort. And wouldn't it be so much easier to just go with the flow? But after having decided to live for Christ fully, we must fight the urge to follow the path of least resistance. It is easy to follow the path of least resistance, and that is what humans naturally do, but we are called to something better.

I spent a little time in the ROTC in college. One of the

things I learned is that ambushes are usually set up on trails and other areas that are the easiest for people to move along. This is because that is where you know the enemy will be traveling. They will be traveling through these areas because humans naturally will choose to walk on a trail over bushwhacking through another. And just like in a combat situation, following the path of least resistance allows opportunities for the Enemy to set ambushes.

Make no mistake: the Enemy doesn't want or like us to live with purpose. Satan would rather we drift through life. It makes his job so much easier. When we are drifting, we are more susceptible to temptation, we are more easily kept distracted by our comfort, and we will not be living out our faith. So expect opposition from the Enemy as you seek to be intentional and live with purpose.

Never give up. Keep going and never look back. Yes, living life without purpose might seem easier and more comfortable, but it is not what we were made for. Keep going with this way of life, for it is better and fuller. It will be a lifelong fight to continue in this way, but it will be worth it. It will get easier, but that will only come after time spent living with purpose.

I love sci-fi movies. In one of my favorite sci-fi comedies, *Galaxy Quest*, one character has a catchphrase: "Never give up; never surrender!" This should be our catch phrase as well, as we seek to live with intention and with purpose.

Tenacity is key. To never give up we must be tenacious. We must be bulldogs: once we bite we won't let go. We must dig in our heels and fight the urge to move from our life of purpose. We need to decide to live for Christ and then decide again and again. This is not for the faint of heart; this is not for someone who is only toying with following Christ. This is for those who know they can't live life for Christ on their

73

own, and so are living in the power of the Holy Spirit. In 1 Corinthians 15:58, it says, "Therefore, my dear brothers, stand firm. Let nothing move you. Always give yourself fully to the work of the Lord, because you know that your labor in the Lord is not in vain." And that is what we need to do. We need to stand firm. Let nothing move you from your pursuit of your Lord and living a life rich in meaning and purpose. We do this because we know it is not in vain; there is a reason for this life. God rewards it. God demands it. God expects it. So let us be resolved. Let us be determined. Let us be persistent. Let us have a drive to live for our Lord. And Lord, help us be steadfast.

Part 3

THE HOW

Chapter 16

INTENTIONAL STANDING: STAND FIRM

The accounts of David's mighty men have always intrigued me. To be called a mighty man is something I believe all men want for themselves. They wish that others would recognize their mightiness, their power, strength, and worth. It is very manly to be mighty. At the end of 2 Samuel, we get a list of the mighty men and their achievements. One of those men stood out to me during my last reading of this passage.

In 2 Samuel 23:11, 12, we find the story of Shammah. He wasn't just included in the list of thirty; he was one of the three main dudes, the mightiest of the mighty. What made this man so mighty? He stood firm.

The story shows the Philistines and the Israelites in conflict. Whether this was a full-blown war or one of the many little conflicts and raids doesn't really matter. Armies were facing off, blades were sharpened, arrows were notched, and war chants were shouted. The armies faced off in a field of lentils. But, when they found themselves face-to-face with the Philistines, it was apparently too much for the Israelite army, because they bolted—all but one man. One man against an army. One man, by himself, against a nation. Shammah stood his ground. He stood firm.

What made Shammah stand his ground? Yes, he was a mighty man. But how did he become mighty? Maybe he was fed up with the Philistines' taking his people's land. Maybe he stood because he was a patriot and said, "Not today, not one more acre, not one more field of Israel will become owned and occupied by these Philistines!" Even a field of lentils was not going to be given over to them. This could be true, and probably was true to some extent. A person doesn't usually join the army unless he or she is a patriot. But I think there was something more.

Could it be, maybe, that these mighty men, all of them, including Shammah, were mighty because they followed David's example? David was mighty, and many enemies fell before him. But he was mighty because he trusted and followed God. So maybe Shammah, when he took his stand, was taking a stand very similar to David's stand against Goliath. A stand not rooted in his own strength, but one rooted in the strength of his God. This was a strength that empowered him to stand against an army. It is a strength that empowers us to stand firm in this life as we follow our God.

The Bible commands us to stand firm. 1 Corinthians 15:58 says, "Therefore, my dear brothers, stand firm. Let nothing move you. Always give yourself fully to the work of the Lord, because you know that your labor in the Lord is not in vain." We are commanded to stand firm, so that when the waves of turmoil and the ranks of opposition come against us, we stand our ground. We don't let these things change our position; we don't let them push us around. We stand firm and let nothing move us. We know what we believe, we know how we are to live, we know the truth, and on these we stand. When popular opinions shift, when the culture's tide changes, we stand firm.

But notice how the verse starts, with that very important word *therefore*. This word points back to what Paul just wrote—that we have a great hope in the resurrection because death has been defeated. We can stand firm because we know that our God wins in the end, we know that the pain is temporary, and we know that there is something far greater waiting for us. We stand because Christ has already won this for us and has assured us that this great end is ours in Him. So, just like Shammah, we stand because we trust and have faith in God—who is bigger than anything we face.

How do we stand firm? We stand firm when our basis for what is true comes from the Word of God and not what we hear on TV. We stand firm when we decide we are living our morals, which are based on the nature of our loving God, and not just following what the culture says is "right" or "acceptable." We stand firm when, for following Christ, people criticize us, call us names, oppress the church, and even persecute the church, but we don't let that change how we follow.

Have you ever noticed that people have unique postures and unique ways they move and stand? I can recognize many friends from their posture and how they are walking or standing even before I can see their face. How you intentionally stand for Christ depends on what is going on in your life. The student might stand differently than the businessperson. The church leader might stand firm in different ways than the person holding public office. But we all stand firm in the truth of Jesus Christ and the Word of God. We all have to take a stand on the truth of who Jesus is and the truth of salvation found in God's Word, the Bible. So, while there might be differences in how we stand, we are all standing firm in the same truth and on the same ground.

Chapter 17

INTENTIONAL SITTING: BE STILL

My son is a handful. He is into everything, talking all the time, begging for attention incessantly, and basically never still. But when he goes silent, or when the house gets quiet, my wife and I know that he is up to something.

Not that long ago, the house was a little too quiet. So I went investigating. And, sure enough, there was my son, up to his elbows in trouble. Literally. He was playing in his fish tank, scooping up the gravel and piling it high in the filter. I think he was trying to pet one of his fish as well. Water was everywhere, his clothes were soaked with fishy water, and the carpet was splattered with the contents of the aquarium. This and many other instances have taught me to fear the quiet when my son is awake.

Many of us, if not most of us, fear the quiet in our everyday lives. We live in a fast-paced culture that doesn't want to stop and reflect. We are encouraged to always be plugged into a device or plopped down in front of a screen. It is as if all of us are afraid of what it might mean if there is quiet. We are afraid of what might happen.

Psalm 46:10 commands, "Be still, and know that I am God." We are commanded to stop and be still, to put down the cell phone, to turn off the TV, to unplug from social media, to take a step back from our checklists and to-do lists, and to simply be still. It is in this stillness that we can know that God is who He has said He is. He is God, the Almighty, Maker, Creator, Designer, Master, Lord, Redeemer, Rescuer, and so much more. It is in stillness, in the quiet, when we can stop our striving that gets us nowhere and come to reflect, ponder, wonder, and meditate on our Lord.

But we don't want to, and we don't see any benefit in this. To take time sitting still seems like a waste of time. It is the opposite of what we have been trained to do, which is strive, achieve, and earn. How can we accomplish anything if we don't do anything? How can we be the best if we don't spend all our time achieving? But maybe that is exactly the point, that to stop and be still will show us the truth that no matter how hard we strive and no matter how hard we work, we can't save ourselves. Speaking to obstinate people, the Lord declared in Isaiah 30:17, "In repentance and rest is your salvation, in quietness and trust is your strength, but you would have none of it." This is not a new development in the history of the world; humans are tainted by sin and so desire to be our own gods. We are deluded enough to think it will work out. But it is in repenting of doing it on our own and in our own way that we find salvation. It is in quietness, a quietness that trusts not in our achievements, but in what Christ achieved for us, that we find strength.

But how will this work? How can being still actually do

something? It is not magic. The Bible makes it very clear that the Lord is the one who leads us to this quietness so that we can come to a place of trust and rest. Psalm 23:2 says, "He makes me lie down in green pastures, he leads me beside quiet waters." God leads us to a place where we know that He is in control, He has our backs, and He provides. In this place it is impossible to think that we can somehow do life on our own or in our own way. We realize we are utterly dependent on God. Zephaniah 3:17 says, "The Lord your God is with you, He is mighty to save. He will take delight in you, He will quiet you with his love, He will rejoice over you with singing." When we come to know the love that God has for us, it quiets our souls, it silences our questions, and it stills our doubts. We know a Love that gave us His Son. We know a Love that walked as one of us. We know a Love that knows the temptations and trials we face. And we know a Love that conquers all to gain us. David Mathis says it like this: "For those of us who are in Christ, we want to come back better—not only rested, but more ready to love and sacrifice. We want to find new clarity, resolve, and initiative, or return primed to redouble our efforts, by faith, in our callings in the home, among friends, at work, and in the body of Christ."[9]

We need to be intentionally sitting, intentionally planning time to be still. It is in this stillness that we remember and remind ourselves who is God and who isn't. It is in this stillness that we can release our anxiety and worries and trust the God who loves us. It is in this stillness that we can examine our doubt and compare it to the truth of Christ.

So how do we do this? We can work it into our times of studying the Bible. As we open our Bibles, we can take a minute to still our thoughts and minds so that we can come

---

9. David Mathis, *Habits of Grace* (Wheaton, IL: Crossway, 2016), 138.

to the Word of God ready to receive. We can also work in times of silence into our regular lives. Turn the radio off every now and then in the car. Let the silence wash over you. Maybe you purposefully engage in times when you unplug from something. Put the cell phone down for a day, don't surf the web for a set time, withdraw for a time from any other thing that can become white noise. Dare to be still with your thoughts and God and see what happens.

Chapter 18

INTENTIONAL WALKING: FOLLOW ME

How did Jesus describe the Christian life? It is an interesting thought and one which needs to be answered by the Gospels. When you look at the Gospels, there seems to be a common motif: Jesus calls for people, which I believe includes you and me, to follow Him. Just a quick count shows Jesus calls others to follow Him around six times each in Matthew and John and five times each in Mark and Luke. To Jesus, to follow was to live for Him.

We live in an age when it seems that belief and action are no longer connected as they should be. We are told not to judge people when we call into question their beliefs because their action or inaction doesn't seem to align with said belief. We are called judgmental and legalistic when we dare question actions and what they say about a person's belief. But Jesus firmly associated belief and action. I dare you to read the

Gospels to see that when Jesus talks about people who believe and love him, those people follow, obey, live a certain way, and do certain things.

We might get a little uncomfortable with these verses because, in evangelical circles, we are concerned about being clear that no one earns their salvation through good deeds or works. So we, rightly, focus on being saved by grace through faith. This is truth, a glorious gospel truth. But the problem comes when we stop there. We ignore that the law is declared good by Paul, the champion of "saved by grace." It is good because, for those of us who are saved, it becomes a guide that helps us follow our Lord. J.I packer puts it this way: "Love and law are not opponents but allies, forming together the axis of true morality."[10] He also says, "Commandment keeping is the only true way to love the Father and the Son."[11] So, yes, we are saved by grace through faith, period. But once we are saved, we are called to follow, to live, to be obedient, and to do.

We are called to intentionally walk through life with purpose, following Jesus.

There are so many verses that address this point that it is, in fact, hard to focus on only a few. I challenge you to take a look through the Bible to see how many verses and passages you can find that speak of this intentional walk. This verse should help get you started:

Since we live by the Spirit, let us keep in step with the Spirit.

—Gal. 5:25

---

10. J.I. Packer, *Growing in Christ* (Wheaton, IL: Crossway, 1994), 232.
11. Ibid., 233.

Discussing how the Christian life is one of living in and by the Spirit, Paul encourages all Christians to keep in step with the Spirit. To live by the Spirit is to live for and to God, it is not to follow the desires of the sinful nature. Paul presents in stark contrast two ways of living: You can either live your life for yourself, following your desires and passions, and if you do so he paints a pretty vivid picture of the result in Galatians 5:19–21. The way of life opposed to the sinful nature is living by the Spirit. And this life is characterized by the fruit of the Spirit. Take a look at this fruit. Is this fruit brought about in idleness or in action? In action, of course. Fruit implies that there was a process, that there was growth, and that people can see the result.

This phrase "keep in step" was used outside of the New Testament to refer to soldiers moving in formation.[12] So we get this picture of Christians marching along with the Spirit, moving with the Spirit or in the Spirit's direction. The Christian's life is one of intentionally moving toward and in the direction of the Spirit. We are called to follow Christ by submitting our lives to His Spirit, whom He sent to us for this purpose.

How can you keep in step with the Spirit? You have to listen to Him. You have to know Him. You have to have Him. All Christians have the Spirit from the moment of conversion, and we should recognize how the Spirit has been working on us to change and regenerate our hearts since that time. Part of this is a change in our affections. Where once we loved ourselves, our pleasures, and following the god of our stomach (Philip. 3:19), we now love Christ, God, the Spirit, and following Him. So we pay attention. We know the truth

---

12. Matthew Harmon, *Philippians: A Mentor Commentary* (London, England: Christian Focus, 2015), 368.

contained in the Word of God so that we can live accordingly. We examine the choices before us and submit them to the very same Word.

I had many friends who were in marching band. I, thankfully, was spared that ordeal. But they always talked about the seriousness the band directors had toward their marching. They had to practice again and again. They were called to be in step with one another. Why? Because if they were not, the whole formation would fall apart, and, in the worst-case scenario, people would run into each other.

So we are called to be in step with the Spirit, to learn how the Spirit would have us walk so we are not tripping through life. This requires being intentional about our choices and actions.

And being intentional also includes not following the crowd. This is what Psalm 1 tells us: the person who doesn't "walk in the counsel of the wicked or stand in the way of sinners or sit in the seat of mockers" is blessed. To intentionally walk through this life following Jesus includes intentionally not following those who are not following Jesus. We do not listen to the counsel of the wicked. We don't associate with the ways of sinners. We don't sit in a group of mockers. This is not a call to separate from them even to the point of not being able to talk with them and share the gospel. But it is a call that to people there is a clear distinction that we don't think, act, or live how they do. Instead, our delight is elsewhere: it is in God's law.

The person who chooses to not associate with people opposed to God will be blessed. This word *blessed* is the Hebrew word *asher* and is better translated as *happy*. This sense of *happy* works better with the phrasing of *delight*. This choice of not following the world (the system of belief that is opposed to God) and following God should not be one which brings us down. If it does, we haven't understood whom we are following at all! Instead, this decision comes because we know that God is more satisfying, more lasting, more everything than the ways of this world. We follow because we know it is better and brings a better life. Charles Spurgeon, preaching on this Psalm, said, "It is an old saying, and possibly a true one, that every man is seeking after happiness. If it is so, then every man should read this Psalm, for this directs us where happiness is to be found in its highest degree and purest form!"[13]

Would how you think about intentionally walking through life by following Jesus change if you realized that this is the way to happiness? Intentionally walk toward true lasting happiness.

---

13. Charles H. Spurgeon, "The Truly Blessed Man" (Sermon #3270)

Chapter 19

INTENTIONAL TIME: BE WITH ME

I recently came home after being gone for a week at a conference. My son, Titus, was of course very excited to see me. So excited that for the next several days he was glued to my side. He wanted to go everywhere I went, and he wanted to be with me at all times. The constant refrain was "Play with me, Daddy!" With that appeal, I just had to. The truth is that all relationships are founded and grounded on time spent with one another.

The common modern expression for this spending time with God is "quiet time." Christians are urged to spend time each day in prayer and reading their Bibles. The thought is that this is one of the basic and fundamental building blocks of the Christian's growth. Greg Ogden says it like this: "One indicator of the depth of our relationship with the Lord is our willingness to spend time alone with him not primarily for what we get out of it but for what it means to him as well."[14] We should seek to spend time with God because it means that we are keeping our relationship alive and well. We are listening to what He has to say, and we are taking our concerns to Him. When we do this, we can rest assured that we will be growing in our faith.

The two common components are Bible and prayer. We read the Bible because that is how we hear from God. He speaks through the truthfulness of His Word. In 2 Timothy 3:16, Paul tells us that all Scripture is breathed out by God; therefore, we know that by reading it we can grow and be trained to live for God. A common cry from people is the desire to hear from God. We can hear from God each and every day! All we have to do is pick up the Bible and read. Sinclair Ferguson said, "If Scripture said it, God said it."[15]

The second component is prayer. Prayer is talking to God. We bring our worries and troubles and lay them at His feet. This is the thrust of Philippians 4:6, 7. In doing so, we have peace that can come only from God, a peace that transcends our understanding. This peace guards us from doubt that our God does what He says He will do. Jesus established the model of praying to God, and we should follow suit.

We do these so that we can experience anew the grace of God. We want God, and we get Him by having a vivid and flourishing relationship with Him. David Mathis puts it like this:

I can flip a switch, but I don't provide the electricity.
I can turn on a faucet, but I don't make the water flow.

---

14. Greg Ogden, *Discipleship Essentials* (Downers Grove, IL: InterVarsity Press, 2007), 35.

15. Sinclair Ferguson, *From the Mouth of God* (East Peoria, IL: Versa Press, 2014), 3.

There will be no light and no liquid refreshment without someone else providing it. And so it is for the Christian with the ongoing grace of God. His grace is essential for our spiritual lives, but we don't control the supply. We can't make the favor of God flow, but He has given us circuits to connect and pipes to open expectantly. There are paths along which He has promised His favor.[16]

To receive God's grace we have to go to Him. To go to Him we have to know Him. And we know Him by having a relationship with Him through Jesus Christ.

There are many excuses a person can give for not having a quiet time. I bet you have given plenty yourself. But these are just excuses. Yes, you might be busy, but we prioritize what is important to us. Yes, you might be under stress at work and home, but that means you should be running to the One that can deal with your stress. Yes, you might be in a spiritual dry spell, but that means you need to be present with the One that gives the rain. It comes down to this: do you want to grow in your faith? I'll let Ogden have the final word: "The questions is whether we will be mediocre Christians or growing Christians. A major factor in determining the answer is whether or not we develop the discipline of a daily quiet time."[17]

---

16. David Mathis, *Habits of Grace* (Wheaton, IL: Crossway, 2016), 25.
17. Ogden, 36.

Chapter 20

INTENTIONAL PLACE: CHURCH

Today many see going to church as optional. The attitude seems to be that church can be good, but is really not a vital or necessary part of the Christian's life. In fact, there are even some movements that have been building for decades that consider organized religion in all its forms to be, at the very least, unnecessary, and maybe even hindering to a person's journey. Even pop stars make comments comparing church attendance to going out to grab tacos.[18]

But when we read the Bible, we get a different picture.

---

18. Justin Bieber in Joe La Puma, "The Deep End," *Complex*, http://religionnews.com/2015/09/29/justin-bieber-you-dont-need-to-go-to-church-to-be-a-christian/.

The picture the New Testament paints is one in which the church is the expression of the people of God. To talk of the people of God was to talk about the church, universal and local, invisible and visible. The sheer number of times the New Testament gives commands that include "one another" stresses and emphasizes the simple fact that we were never made to live the journey alone. The Christian game is a team sport, not a solo show. We forget this at our peril. To lose sight of this handicaps us. Too many of us go through life limping because we forget that God has put others in our lives to lean on. We lose sight that there is a whole community that exists to help us follow Christ and live as He commands, and it helps us glorify our Lord. Thom Rainer says it this way: "God did not give us local churches to become country clubs where membership means we have privileges and perks. He placed us in churches to serve, to care for others, to pray for leaders, to learn, to teach, to give, and, in some cases, to die for the sake of the gospel."[19]

In Psalm 92:12, 13, the psalmist describes the righteous as trees "planted in the house of the Lord." This is an interesting phrase and points back to the blessed man of Psalm 1, being a tree by streams of water. We are to be planted in the house of the Lord. If we were to apply this to our context, it could be argued that we are to be planted in a church. It is only by being in a local church for an extended time that our roots are put down, meaning that relationships have been built and people can speak the truth into our lives. This would also argue against hopping from one church to another, since a tree transplanted again and again doesn't do so well. I would say this can be used as an encouragement that by being in a Bible-believing and Bible-teaching church for

---

19. Thom S. Rainer, *I Am a Church Member* (Nashville: B&H, 2013), 6.

a prolonged time helps us mature and become strong like a "cedar of Lebanon."

The Bible makes it very clear that the church is supposed to be a place where the wisdom of God is proclaimed (Eph. 3:10) because it is the "pillar and foundation of the truth" (1 Tim. 3:15). Where can people today get truth? The church is where. People have a tendency to look almost anywhere else, and we have to call them and ourselves back to the true wellspring of truth. The church is the place where wisdom and truth are proclaimed because it is where the Bible is opened and proclaimed. It is the place where the body of Christ gathers together and praises His name. It is the place that seeks to make known the reality that Jesus Christ is the Messiah, the Savior, and our Lord. If this is true, then shouldn't we be there?

The church, as a family, should gather around every brother and sister that is a part of the community. It is the community life that gives the church so much good influence on the life of the average believer. Ed Shaw says, "When the church feels like a family, I can cope with not ever having my own partner and children."[20] Shaw was speaking about a specific issue, but I believe that most relational, personal problems can be addressed by the church. The church acting and living as a family helps us be encouraged when we are down. It can help us check ourselves when we are out of line. It can direct us to new ways of seeing the Word of God. It can motivate us to new heights of worship. It can give us a place in which we can serve not only believers, but the community as a whole.

With all these benefits that come with the church, shouldn't

---

20. Ed Shaw, *Same-Sex Attraction and the Church* (Downers Grove, IL: InterVarsity, 2015), 48.

we seek to be intentional about our involvement? This means that we plan to attend. We plan to sing. We plan to listen and take notes. We plan to put application into action in our lives. Join with your family in Christ.

Chapter 21

KEEP THE HEART

The idea of being intentional is not a new thought. It is a thought that has been around since the beginning of our faith. It is an idea and concept that Christians have been wrestling with since the beginning. It has been a subject of sermons and books since there have been churches. One great example is the puritan John Flavel's work *Keeping the Heart*.

A puritan pastor in the 1600s, John Flavel had a passion for the Christian community to be intentional in their faith and practice. To Flavel, the issue was to be diligent in the "heart work" of our faith. This is the idea that the heart is the core of who we are; therefore, we need to live out the change of heart that comes when someone is regenerated by the Holy Spirit.

What does it mean to keep the heart as John Flavel would have us do? He describes it as this: "The constant care and diligence of such a renewed man to preserve his soul in that holy frame to which grace has raised it."[21] This definition is another way to talk about living intentionally. It describes much of what has been written in this book and the ideas that I have tried to express. Let's take a look at this definition of keeping the heart and see where it leads us.

Before we dive into this definition, though, we must recognize that it is based on Scripture. Flavel didn't just come up with this on his own; it is what he saw as the application of the Word of God in his life. Consider Proverbs 4:23, which says, "Above all else, guard your heart, for it is the wellspring of life." Flavel uses the King James translation which says "keep thy heart." This is a command found in Scripture to make sure our heart, that core of who we are and from which all of our desires, thoughts, discernments come, is guarded, kept for Christ. This would take some intentional action.

Flavel understands that this needs to be intentional. He uses the words *care* and *diligence*, which show that the actions needed to keep the heart are intentional choices to not only understand the problem, but act on it. Not only that, but these are to be constant. It is not a once-in-a-while kind of effort, but a pattern. We need to have constant (regular and ongoing) care about our heart. So often people act without thinking, they speak without filtering, and they make up their minds without any processing. But what we are encouraged to do here is to check our hearts and care about what we find in them. And we are to do this with diligence. To me, that word brings up images or thoughts of someone on top of the situation. Nothing is going to catch them by surprise. And that is how we are to be with our hearts: we know who we

---

21. John Flavel, *Keeping the Heart* (Ross-Shire, Great Britain: Christian Focus, 2012), 18.

are and what is going on so well that we can deal with issues when they are still minor. We have diligence.

To keep the heart means that the Christian perseveres. That means we keep at what we know we need to keep at. We stay true to what God has called us to. We keep going. No matter what is thrown our way or what comes up, we hold true to our Lord and persevere. To persevere means to be intentional in what we do and how we do it so that we can keep going. We intentionally hold on to our Lord. We intentionally keep doing what we have been told to do. We intentionally avoid what we have been told to avoid.

All is to keep us in fellowship with God. Now, don't misunderstand what Flavel is saying here. He is not saying that our standing with God is in question. No, not at all. He is saying that if we don't keep the heart, our fellowship might be in question. Our standing depends totally on God, He saved us and, as Flavel says, "raised us." That is never in question. But we, sinful humans that we are, can live in such a way that our communion or fellowship with God is hindered or weakened. We want thriving fellowship with God so that we can live life to the fullest right now, as faithful servants living for our Lord in all we do.

Keeping the heart can only happen if we are already believers. As Flavel says, "to keep the heart, necessarily supposes a previous work of regeneration, which has set the heart right, by giving it a new spiritual inclination, for as long as the heart is not set right by grace as to its habitual frame, no means can keep it right with God."[22] And not only do we rely on the Spirit to regenerate us so that we can keep the heart, we rely on the Spirit to empower us so that we can do the work of keeping the heart. Flavel says that "the duty is ours,

---

22. Ibid., 17.

though the power is of God; what power we have depends upon the exciting and assisting strength of Christ."[23] People can hear about keeping the heart or living intentionally and feel as if it is all up to how well they can follow rules or do what they need to do. When we have that mindset, we have failed before we start. God gives us the power. On our own, we couldn't live for Him, but because He gives us His Spirit, we can. Keep the heart, knowing that God gives you what you need to do so.

So, what do we do to keep the heart? Flavel doesn't say anything that you haven't heard before. We do this by doing the basic disciplines of the Christian life. We pray, we read our Bibles, we are in relationships with other Christians who hold us accountable, we are in church, and we seek to apply what we know from the Word of God. To live intentionally or to keep the heart is not some special formula; it is being diligent in what we know we are called to do.

So how are you going to keep your heart for God?

---

23. Ibid., 15.

Chapter 22

PRESS ON

The reality is that being intentional takes work, and work takes energy, and energy is all-too-easily drained. So how can we keep after God, even when we feel used up and drained? I think Paul gives us some good insight in Philippians 3:12–4:1. Let's read this passage and then see how that addresses how we all too often feel.

The repeated command is to press on. He presses on to take hold of that for which Christ Jesus took hold of him. The word translated *press on* is *dioko*, and it is the same word that Paul uses earlier to describe how he persecuted the church. The result is a subtle wordplay that is impossible to bring into English.[24] In effect Paul says that he devotes the same sort of intense energy and effort that he once directed toward

---

24. Matthew Harmon, *Philippians: A Mentor Commentary* (Ross-Shire, Great Britain: Christian Focus, 2015), 352.

persecuting the church into now pursuing progress in being made into the image of Christ.

The phrasing of "take hold" also gives a sense of overtaking something being chased. To take hold of something carries the image of chasing it down and bringing it to ground. When I think of that, two images come to mind. A lion chasing a gazelle and a dog chasing a ball. The lion needs the gazelle to live; therefore, chasing God is a matter of life and death for us. The dog chases the ball out of pure joy; therefore, we should chase after God because we know that He is the source of all joy. All this language gives a sense of intensity. This isn't something done halfheartedly, but something done with conviction and effort. Press on!

I love how Paul phrased this, that Christ Jesus took hold of him first. The only reason that Paul is able to press forward to make perfection his own is that Christ has first made Paul His own. The order is essential because it places emphasis on the initiative of divine grace and election as the foundation for Paul's pursuit of growth in holiness. We can apply this to ourselves, and to the Christian life, and say that Christ has already made the believer His own; as a result, the believer presses forward to the perfection that is not yet his, but will one day come at the resurrection. When we put it all together, the picture is of Christ pursuing and overtaking the sinner who is running away from Him so Christ can make him His own. Then the sinner's heart is changed, his affections turned to Christ who then leads him to pursue the final goal of perfection. We pursue because Christ has already pursued and caught us.

Paul describes how that is done. We forget what is behind and strain toward the goal and prize. Paul says that he forgets what is behind, the failures and the successes. The point is that the past doesn't have the power to make him more like Christ. The past still has an effect, but it doesn't define us or shape our identity. That comes from Christ, and we are called to respond anew each day.

Forget the past. Those failures, they can haunt us, I know, but they don't define us. I have to tell myself this because I have some failures in my past. I was fired from being a pastor, and if I dwell on it, I'll let this failure define me. But I forget it. We also forget the successes. We don't rest on our laurels. We say good job, way to go—and press on today.

We strain toward what is ahead, which carries the sense of exerting oneself to the uttermost. This is athletic imagery drawn from Greco-Roman footraces. Paul is portraying himself as a runner who strains toward the goal of the finish line. Matthew Harmon adds this insight:

> Trained runners know that looking back not only slows one down, but more significantly takes one's eyes off the goal, which can lead to disaster. Indeed, one of the tricks of running I learned as a young athlete was to lock my eyes onto a runner who was in front of me. If my focus remained on that runner, gradually over time I would find myself closing in on him, as my body naturally adjusted its pace to catch him. Perhaps in a similar fashion, Paul envisions himself running the Christian race, with his eyes fixed on Christ, straining toward the finish line.[25]

In verse 17, Paul then switches to the very practical command to follow his example and also take note of those who are. There are two commands, to follow Paul and also to follow others. We hesitate at these commands, because it sounds arrogant to us. But Paul is not being arrogant.

---

25. Ibid., 357.

He just admitted that he wasn't perfect. But he knows that he is following Christ, so he can say confidently, "Where you see Christ, follow. Where you don't see Christ, move on." He says that there are others who are living according to the pattern he gave them, so follow them too. Paul is not alone. There are people who follow God and live out their faith. All believers should take note of these people and follow them. We should take stock of who is influencing us and who we are following.

Paul closes this section with the gentle, pastoral encouragement that this is how they should stand firm in the Lord. How? By pressing on. By following his example and those who live for God's pattern of life. By awaiting and trusting in the return of Christ. All of this—this allows us to stand firm. To press on through whatever life throws at us.

So press on toward Christ. Little-by-little, one step at a time, press on. You want to stand firm? Then press on. You want to be solid? Then live intentionally. It is not a gimmick or a get-rich-quick scheme. It takes all of who we are and all of our lives to do, but it is worth it. Let's live intentionally.

Chapter 23

D.E.C.I.D.E.D.

Have you decided to live life on purpose with intentionality in all you do? I hope you have. You have made it to the end of the book, and I hope you have been encouraged and have seen the importance of living with purpose. It is hard. It takes effort. But it starts with a decision on your part to rise above the standard of this world and live wholeheartedly for Christ. I now invite you into the ranks of the D.E.C.I.D.E.D.

This is not a club or an organization, but rather a simple tool that describes the person who has made a decision to live a life on purpose for Christ. This word seeks to describe and explain some of the character qualities needed and the actions required. It is one way of looking at this issue, not the only way.

D. Decide to have an intentional life. It all starts with a decision. You have to make one: not making a decision is making a decision. It is my hope that now, at the end of this journey, you decide every day to live a big life for Christ.

We make hundreds, if not thousands, of decisions daily, most of them without thinking or really processing. So, in a way, we have to decide how we are going to make decisions. We have to decide that our decisions are going to be honoring to the Lord and that we will use Scripture as our basis and foundation.

E. Expect what is to come with this decision, the good and the bad. Expect that your life can be fuller, with more meaning. Expect that you will know that your life has a purpose and that all the little bits in between have purpose as well. But also expect that there will be sacrifice and there will be things given up. Expect that this could be a hard journey where you might stumble and fall every now and then. And finally, expect that your life will be more on track with what the Lord desires as you walk with purpose.

In a way, Christianity is an expectant faith. We expect that the Spirit is working in us. We expect good gifts and blessings from the Father. We expect the return and final victory of Jesus. We are expectant. And this being expectant is a trust that God is going to do what He said He was going to do. It is a trust that we can rely on Him. Being expectant is having faith. We have faith that living with purpose will be for the better. We have the trust that God's way of life is better than our way of life.

C. Consideration is a must. Just as you expect good and bad, now you consider what is going to happen. We are called to walk with intent, and that requires actually considering outcomes of actions and consequences of thoughts. It takes consideration to navigate this world with purpose. Let us spend some time and consider how our actions must change.

We do this so they will not catch us by surprise. Let us consider how our thoughts about life and what we do must change. Let us consider our relationships and how they can help or hinder us in living a big life for Christ. Too often we live without first considering what is going on or what might happen. So let us have consideration.

Too often I can act without thinking. And this can lead to bad results. But the considerate person spends time processing and thinking through what might happen. When I was younger, I was hanging out with some friends, and we came upon a waterfall with a pool at the bottom. The pool looked deep and the water was clear. It was begging for us to jump in. And so I did. I leaped without considering what could happen. The pool wasn't as deep as it appeared, and I hit the bottom rather hard. I was lucky that I didn't seriously hurt myself. We can be like that in life. We leap and get scratched up a little, but since we haven't seriously hurt ourselves, we keep doing it. Let us consider before we leap.

I. Do you have Insight? It takes hard work to be self-reflective. This usually happens best when you have a friend or mentor walking alongside you who can look at your life from the outside. This person then can speak with insight into how you have grown, as well as how you might still need to grow. This process is not for you alone; it has to be worked out in your community. You need intelligent, intimate insight, so that you can see your progress and continue to grow.

Our culture doesn't make this easy. We are told to be islands unto ourselves. That is not how we were designed to live. We were designed for community with God and with each other. It might be hard developing those relationships that can give insight, but it is worth it. Your pride or ego might take a hit or two, but it is worth it. You will have to be vulnerable, which no one likes to be, but it is worth it.

D. Be Determined! Without determination, this whole endeavor will crumble. When the going gets tough or our laziness naturally kicks in, we need determination to keep us on track. Are you determined? Are you ready to keep going, even when you will not feel like it? You must. If this is to work, you have to be determined.

One of the things I love about my young son is how determined he can be. He wants to do things himself without any help. There have been times when he has decided that he will put his own shoes on and refuses to let me help him. He sits there, determined to master how they go on and fit his feet. When I try to reach in to help, he knocks my hands away. That is one determined boy. We need to have that same determination. Not that we won't accept help, but that we won't give up. We keep after it, even when it doesn't seem to be working.

E. Are you Excited yet? Get ready to be excited, because you will see progress as you grow. You need to be excited about what is going to happen and how your life will change. Christ is the One working in you. This is a gradual process, for the most part. But when you look back after a little while and see where you were and where you are now, you should be excited. Someone could be reading about this idea of living with purpose, and think that it is sounds like work—and hard work at that. What we need to realize is that there is excitement in this idea. The same excitement parents have when their kid takes that first step should be present in us as we take steps to grow in living with purpose. It is exciting to live out our faith and follow our Lord.

D. Dedicate your life to Christ and the pursuit of Him. To live for Christ with purpose in all we do takes dedication. It takes commitment. It takes someone giving all of who they are over to Christ. When we dedicate our lives to Christ, we are saying that He is our all, He is our Lord. We are declaring to ourselves that He owns us and we must follow. We, with intention, remove ourselves from the lordship of our lives and submit to our rightful Lord, Christ. We place ourselves under His Word, to follow where it would lead us. We place ourselves in His body, the church, serving and being fed. We organize our time so that Bible reading and prayer is a priority. We cultivate friendships and relationships with the express purpose of God using them. If we are dedicated, our whole lives are given over to Christ.

So are you D.E.C.I.D.E.D.? We all want to have a big life for Christ. It is a noble desire and a great motivation to have. But we can only get there when we are intentional with our lives and realize that we should be living with purpose in all we do.

ABOUT THE AUTHOR

Adam Kareus is a pastor at River Valley Community Church in Fort Smith, Arkansas. Adam and his beautiful wife Kacee have a wild little boy, Titus, and a new baby girl, Jillian. Adam earned his Master of Divinity from Denver Seminary and has been serving in pastoral roles on churches' staffs since 2009.